CLASSIC STEAM

JOHN CORKILL & PETER HANSON

CLASSIC STEAM

JOHN CORKILL & PETER HANSON

Steam at work

Compiled by Chris Banks

SLP

Silver Link Publishing Ltd

First published in February 1995

British Library Cataloguing in Publication Data

A catalogue record for this book is available from the British Library.

ISBN 1 85794 044 X

Those photographs taken by John Corkill are identified by the letters *JC*, those taken by Peter Hanson by the letters *PH*.

Silver Link Publishing Ltd
Unit 5
Home Farm Close
Church Street
Wadenhoe
Peterborough PE8 5TE
Tel/fax (0832) 720440

Printed and bound in Great Britain

Frontispiece Looking in: Liverpool Bank Hall-based 'Jubilee' 4-6-0 No 45698 *Mars* on Edge Hill shed in April 1965. *JC*

Below Closely observed by a young steam admirer, the crew mount their engine, 'Princess Coronation' Class 4-6-2 No 46243 *City of Lancaster*, at Liverpool Lime Street, ready to take a southbound service on Saturday 9 September 1961. The excitement of the journey ahead is admirably captured in this atmospheric study - you can almost hear the roar of the safety valve and smell the hot oil and smoke! *JC*

Contents

A view inside the older part of Liverpool Edge Hill depot in 1965. Fairburn 2-6-4T No 42296 from Lostock Hall raises steam with all the debris of steam working around. Imagine the dangers for shed staff having to pick their way along the coal-strewn aisles in dim lighting at night. No 42296 was a relatively new engine, having been built at Derby and entering traffic at Bradford Low Moor in November 1947, one of the last LMS engines built. It transferred to Lostock Hall during the week-ended 30 July 1949 and remained there until withdrawal during the week-ended 31 July 1965. JC

Introduction

The idea for this book began with a letter from John and Peter to Silver Link Publishing suggesting that the photographs they had taken could form another title in the 'Classic Steam' series. I was subsequently invited to meet our photographers at SLP Editor Will Adams's house in deepest Northamptonshire. No one could doubt where the pair came from, for their Liverpool accents gave it away. On seeing the photographs for the first time, it was apparent that they should be seen and enjoyed by a wider audience, so the seeds were sown for what is now this volume.

Peter Hanson started work for British Railways on Monday 7 September 1953. Along with a number of other eager youngsters he reported to the offices of the District Goods Manager alongside Liverpool Exchange station and was sent to work in the ex-CLC Brunswick Goods Depot delivery office. In May 1955 National Service called, and Peter joined the RAF, only to be found to be medically unfit after two weeks. So, back to the railway, but this time to the ex-GWR premises at Birkenhead Morpeth Docks Goods offices.

Further moves then took place until, in February 1957, Peter started working at the freight accounts section at Liverpool Waterloo Dock. Working through various departments, he gained experience in many areas of accounting until the fateful day in April 1967 when, during the night, a fire reduced the offices to a burned-out wreck. Peter's section relocated to Liverpool Lime Street Chambers, and in 1968 took up residence in a new building alongside Lime Street station, known as Rail House.

Over the next 15 years or so the whole of the British Rail accountancy structure went through many re-organisations, and Peter found himself working at Manchester, then Crewe in the Finance Manager's (Operations) Office, which dealt with area budgets for the London Midland Region. The circle was complete when Peter returned to work in Liverpool in 1989 in the area management team for Merseyside. In April 1994 he became a management accounting assistant in the new Merseyrail Electrics operating unit.

John Corkill started work in August 1957 at Edge Hill shed as an apprentice fitter, working on a daily basis with the steam locomotives. He then followed his career by working at Crewe Works from September 1961 until May 1962. A return to Edge Hill then came about for the rest of 1962, working on his own on engine wash-out duties; this important responsibility was overseen by the foreman, who made sure that the work was carried out correctly.

In January 1963 John was sent over to Sutton Oak shed at St Helens as a need arose for a fitter; there he worked with far less glamorous locomotives, as Sutton Oak was mainly a freight depot. However, experience was gained on locomotive types not allocated to Edge Hill, such as the Ivatt 2-6-2Ts, WD 'Austerity' 2-8-0s and Standard 2-6-0s in the number series 76075 to 76079. One interesting duty was the special examination and attention that John and his colleague fitters had to give to the Willesden Class '5MT' 4-6-0 that would work on to the shed every day to later haul the Pilkington company train of glass products.

The lure of the main-line shed beckoned, and John returned to Edge Hill in April 1963, taking up a vacancy on the three-shift system dealing with running repairs, steam testing after wash-outs, and the daily testing of the Automatic Warning Systems fitted to the locomotives. Now John was again working with the top-link Stanier 'Pacifics' in their final year of activity. The sad decline in the steam locomotive was witnessed at first hand, and tested the fitters' skills to the extreme in keeping what remained in working order.

When Edge Hill closed on 6 May 1968, John accepted transfer to Allerton diesel and electric depot, working in much cleaner conditions but with none of the magic of steam traction. He still works at Allerton, which now repairs and repaints diesel shunters from all over the system.

Both John and Peter had an enthusiasm for the railway, which resulted in the photographs we see here. They met together in 1980 when out photographing steam specials on the Settle & Carlisle line. While discussing the research for this book, to their surprise they realised that they had shared an RCTS trip to Doncaster on 28 February 1960, their respective photographs bringing this to light.

So now settle back and indulge in the nostalgia of a past way of life that will never be seen again. Reflect on what has gone, but rejoice in what is still to be seen through the efforts of the preservationists. The memories of Edge Hill still linger in the minds of those who shared its daily work, and the thrill of photographing steam locomotives carrying out their everyday duties will never be extinguished. All this and more is recorded in the pages of this book. Enjoy it!

Chris Banks
Hinckley, 1995

London Paddington on Tuesday 8 August 1961. 'King' Class 4-6-0 No 6020 *King Henry IV* awaits departure and the placing of a second lamp on the buffer beam to denote an express passenger working to Birmingham and Wolverhampton. The engine was based at Stafford Road shed and is looking somewhat uncared for and dirty, a far cry from when the 'Kings' were the pride of the Great Western fleet. The Class was built between 1927 and 1930 to a design by Collett, and No 6020 was subsequently fitted with a four-row superheater to improve performance, being power-rated '8P' by British Railways. The whole Class was withdrawn in 1962, No 6020 going in July, still allocated to Wolverhampton. *JC*

1. Steam at work: Great Western

Above The 'platform-enders' at Paddington record the engine numbers on 8 August 1961 as '61XX' 2-6-2T No 6163, allocated to Old Oak Common, prepares to leave with empty stock from an earlier arrival. In the background is a 'Britannia' 'Pacific', probably on a Cardiff working. The '61XX' 2-6-2Ts were lively engines and the majority were to be found in the London Division. No 6163 first entered traffic at Truro in October 1935, but ended its days at Southall in October 1965. After a time in storage, it was cut up in February 1966 at Birds yard, Risca. *JC*

Right Exeter St David's station on Thursday 30 July 1959. 'Castle' Class 4-6-0 No 5075 *Wellington* backs down on to an express to take it on to Plymouth and Penzance. The train had been brought in by another 'Castle', No 5032 *Usk Castle*. *Wellington* was allocated new to Wolverhampton Stafford Road in August 1938 and was a Chester engine for most of the 1950s. By 1959 it was based at Exeter and was withdrawn in September 1962 from Bristol St Philips Marsh. In this photograph the engine still retains the original tapered buffers. *PH*

Above We now move to the classic location on the sea wall at Teignmouth. Holidaymakers stroll along by the sea on 30 July 1959 as 'Hall' Class 4-6-0 No 4967 *Shirenewton Hall* rounds the curve on a Plymouth to Birmingham express composed of ex-LMS stock. No 4967 dated from 1929 and spent many years allocated to Bristol St Philips Marsh. Withdrawal came in September 1962 from Swansea Landore. *PH*

Below Looking in the opposite direction at Teignmouth on the same day. 'Castle' Class 4-6-0 No 5079 *Lysander* negotiates the curves along the seawall with a Manchester to Penzance train. *Lysander* entered traffic in May 1939 and went new to Old Oak Common. During the 1950s it was a Newton Abbot engine and remained there until withdrawal in May 1960. *PH*

Right The impressive and powerful appearance of 'King' Class 4-6-0 No 6004 *King George III* is shown to great effect at Teignmouth on that same Thursday. This is a Penzance working and the 'King' is a Plymouth Laira engine, which would be replaced by a 'Castle' at Plymouth. The holidaymakers are not really interested in the passing of another train - but imagine the mass gathering today if this scene was repeated! *PH*

Below A final look at Teignmouth on 30 July 1959. 'Castle' Class 4-6-0 No 5055 *Earl of Eldon*, with the crew enjoying the sea air, passes by with a clean exhaust on the up 'Devonian' from Kingswear to Bradford. No 5055 first took to the rails in June 1936 at Old Oak Common, and spent most of its working life based in London. Withdrawal came in September 1964 from Gloucester Horton Road. *PH*

Above Newton Abbot station on 30 July 1959. 'Hall' Class 4-6-0 No 4944 *Middleton Hall* is ready to leave on an eastbound cross-country express; today this would be an HST working, or even a two-coach Class '158' diesel set. No 4944 was an Exeter engine at this time and dated back to 1929. Withdrawal came in September 1962 from Southall. *PH*

Below The '51XX' 2-6-2T Class dated back to 1903 to a design by Churchward. A further batch, numbered 4100 to 4179, were built under Collett and later Hawksworth from 1935 into the nationalisation era to 1949. This example, No 4174, was one of the 20 engines built in British Railways days. It entered traffic in November 1949 at Cheltenham depot and ended its days at Severn Tunnel Junction in June 1964. This view is at the east end of Newton Abbot station on the same day, with No 4174 awaiting duty. *PH*

Above We move into Cornwall for this scene, recorded a couple of days earlier on Monday 27 July 1959 at St Erth. '45XX' Class 2-6-2T No 4570 runs in from Penzance shed for duty on the St Ives branch. The engine was one of a batch built in November 1924 to an original Churchward design, and numbered 4500 to 4574; nearly all the Class numbered below 4555 had gone by 1959. No 4570 was a survivor until 1963, being withdrawn in January from Plymouth Laira and cut up at Cashmores, Newport, in August 1964. *PH*

Below That Monday was a lovely summer day, as evidenced by this view of another '45XX' Class 2-6-2T, this time No 4559. The location is Wadebridge in North Cornwall, and the working is an afternoon service to Bodmin Road. No 4559 was a St Blazey engine for many years and was withdrawn from there in October 1960. Scrapping was carried out at Woodhams, Barry, in May 1961. Passenger services to Wadebridge ceased from 30 January 1967 when only a freight line remained. Today there is no railway to be seen; the only evidence that a railway existed is the old goods shed, which is now used as an Arts Centre, and part of the main station building, which is retained for the retired residents of the area. *PH*

Hollinswood Bank, south of Oakengates, is the setting for the next three photographs, all taken in May 1962. This was the last summer of the 'Kings' and No 6011 *King James I* climbs with ease on the 11.10 am Paddington to Birkenhead; engines would be changed at Shrewsbury for less regal power. *King James I* ceased operation from Old Oak Common in December 1962 and was one of the last four to remain active. *PH*

Right As a contrast, Wolverhampton Oxley-based 'Grange' Class 4-6-0 No 6830 *Buckenhill Grange* makes a fine sight climbing the bank on a heavy mixed freight for Shrewsbury. No 6830 entered traffic in August 1937 at Newport Ebbw Junction and, after serving at various depots, including Bristol St Philips Marsh for most of the 1950s, was withdrawn from Oxley in October 1965. *PH*

Below The 1.10 pm Paddington to Chester express, with Wolverhampton Stafford Road 'Castle' No 5022 *Wigmore Castle* in charge, climbs Hollinswood Bank in fine style. Even as late as this, 'Castles' were still performing to a high standard and deputising on very tight schedules for failed diesels. Built in August 1932 and going new to Old Oak Common, No 5022 dropped its fire for the last time at Stafford Road in June 1963. *PH*

We next move to Gresford Bank on Saturday 5 October 1963, to find 'Grange' Class 4-6-0 No 6831 *Bearley Grange* in filthy condition and without a shedplate (which should be 2B Oxley) climbing with a freight from Chester. No 6831 went new to Banbury in August 1937 but spent most of its British Railways days at Birkenhead. Withdrawal came in October 1965 from Oxley. *PH*

Above Leamington Spa on Saturday 15 September 1962. The 'Cambrian Coast Express' has just arrived and prepares to leave for London with double-chimneyed 'Castle' Class 4-6-0 No 7036 *Taunton Castle* in charge. This was a relatively young engine, having been built by British Railways in August 1950 and going new to Old Oak Common, where it remained until withdrawal in September 1963. Note the large piece of coal beside the track in the foreground that has fallen from the tender of another locomotive. This could be dangerous for permanent way men, but a bonus to residents with coal fires and houses close to railway lines. *PH*

Right The date is Saturday 26 September 1964 and the Special for the Annual General Meeting of the Talyllyn Railway Society is double-headed by 'Manor' Class 4-6-0 No 7827 *Lydham Manor*, British Railways owned, and privately owned preserved '45XX' 2-6-2T No 4555. The location is near the present Llangollen Railway Deeside loop on the line from Ruabon through Llangollen and Corwen to the Cambrian line and Barmouth. Pat Whitehouse, who died in 1993, had purchased No 4555, the last active member of its class, direct from British Railways when it was withdrawn from Plymouth Laira depot in November 1963. Tyseley shed then became the engine's home for restoration to pre-1948 green livery. No 7827 entered traffic in December 1950, initially going to Chester ex-GWR shed. Withdrawal came in October 1965 from Shrewsbury shed. This engine was also saved for preservation and can now be seen, together with No 4555, on the Paignton & Dartmouth Steam Railway. *PH*

On the Cambrian line on Saturday 6 October 1962, Class '2251' 0-6-0 No 2214 begins the descent of Talerddig Bank with the Machynlleth breakdown train heading back to its home depot. No 2214 had been added to stock in June 1940 at Taunton depot, where it remained until October 1954 when transfer took place to Swindon, then to Didcot the following month. It moved on to Shrewsbury in May 1960, then Machynlleth in September of the same year, final withdrawal taking place in May 1965 after transfer to store at Exmouth Junction. *PH*

The approach to Llandrillo station on Saturday 13 October 1962, with 'Manor' Class 4-6-0 No 7811 *Dunley Manor* on the 2.38 pm Barmouth to Ruabon. Llandrillo and the line from Morfa Mawddach to Ruabon closed on 18 January 1965. No 7811 lasted a little longer, being withdrawn in July of the same year from Cardiff East Dock shed. *PH*

Another 'Manor', this time No 7828 Odney Manor, which was withdrawn from Shrewsbury in September 1965, but can still be enjoyed in preservation. It is here seen leaving Bettisfield station on its way to Whitchurch, the next stop being the delightfully named Fenn's Bank. The train is the through coaches from Aberystwyth, leaving Bettisfield at 4.12 pm and arriving at Whitchurch at 4.29 pm. Local passengers used to walk along the track rather than use the road to the village; such was the way of rural lines. The date of the photograph is Saturday 26 September 1964. The station and line closed two months later on 23 November. PH

Above A 'King' at rest. No 6013 *King Henry VIII* waits at Swindon station to take over a Paddington working on Sunday 22 March 1959. It had been through Swindon Works in February for its last overhaul and is shown here in its final form with double chimney, mechanical lubricator, and four-row superheater. Withdrawal came in June 1962 from Wolverhampton Stafford Road. *PH*

Below A 'King' in action. No 6000 *King George V* approaches Ruabon station with the annual Talyllyn Railway Society Special on Saturday 29 September 1962, one of its last workings for British Railways before withdrawal. After coming off the train at Ruabon it worked back to

Wolverhampton Stafford Road shed via Shrewsbury. It was booked to work light engine back to Old Oak Common in the evening. However, 'Western' Class diesel-hydraulic No D1008 *Western Harrier*, which had only been in traffic for two weeks, failed near Stafford Road while working the 6.40 pm Shrewsbury to Paddington. No 6000 was summoned to bank the train into the station and was then placed at the head with D1008, working right through to Paddington. Retirement for No 6000 came in December along with the other surviving members of the Class, Nos 6011 *King James I*, 6018 *King Henry VI* and 6025 *King Henry III*, all based at Old Oak Common. No 6000 lives on, happily, in preservation. *PH*

The full beauty of the 'Castle' Class 4-6-0 is reflected in this view of No 7029 *Clun Castle*, another escapee into preservation. It has just arrived at Birkenhead Woodside station on Sunday 5 March 1967 with a special that ran to mark the end of through services between Birkenhead and London Paddington. No 7029 was built after nationalisation and took to the rails in May 1950 at Newton Abbot. *JC*

2. Steam at work: Southern

Right Waterloo station on a sunny Monday 5 September 1966. 'West Country' Class 4-6-2 No 34013 *Okehampton* looks in fine condition at the head of the 'Bournemouth Belle' Pullman service. Built in October 1945, No 34013 was first allocated to Exmouth Junction. Rebuilt to the form as shown here in October 1957, withdrawal came in July 1967 from Salisbury, which was the last month of Southern steam working. *JC*

Below Waterloo two days later, with 'Merchant Navy' 4-6-2 No 35023 awaiting departure on an express to Weymouth. Formerly named *Holland-Afrika Line*, the nameplates had been removed for future sale. This engine also survived until July 1967 and was withdrawn from Nine Elms. *JC*

A powerful shot of 'Merchant Navy' No 35028 awaiting departure at Waterloo with a train for Southampton on Monday 12 June 1967. This was another case of the nameplates (*Clan Line*) having been removed for safe keeping. When this photograph was taken Waterloo was the last London station to see daily steam working, and it seemed unbelievable that in only a few more weeks this would all be history. *Clan Line* can of course still be seen in preservation, once more re-united with its nameplates. *JC*

Above The early evening light illuminates 'Merchant Navy' Class 4-6-2 No 35030 *Elder Dempster Lines* as it runs into Wareham in September 1966 on an up express. Allocated to Weymouth at the time, it was withdrawn in July 1967 from Nine Elms and was the last active member of the Class. JC

Right With its banshee whistle wailing at full blast, unrebuilt 'West Country' Class 4-6-2 No 34023 *Blackmoor Vale*, also now preserved, hurtles through Eastleigh station on a Waterloo train on Thursday 8 September 1966. No 34023 had first entered traffic in February 1946 at Ramsgate and was another survivor in British Railways service until July 1967, finishing at Nine Elms. JC

Left Making a lot of noise and impatient to go, 'Battle of Britain' Class 4-6-2 No 34071 *601 Squadron* waits for the road at Farnborough on Wednesday 7 September 1966. The driver looks up at the blowing safety valve anticipating an exhilarating run with a willing engine. With the coming end of steam on the Southern, crews were eager to 'have a go', and three-figure speeds were regularly recorded from the autumn of 1966 through to the following summer. Nineteen rebuilt and two unrebuilt members of the Bulleid 'West Country' and 'Battle of Britain' Classes of 'Pacific' lasted through to the final days of Southern steam. No 34071 didn't quite make it, for it was withdrawn from Eastleigh shed in April 1967. JC

Below left Southampton in the rain on Saturday 21 August 1965. 'Merchant Navy' Class 4-6-2 No 35014 *Nederland Line* has just taken water prior to leaving on its journey to Bournemouth. This engine was commissioned for service at Nine Elms in February 1945 and ended its career based at Weymouth in March 1967. JC

Above We now cross over to the Isle of Wight on 21 August 1965 for the following sequence of photographs. An 'O2' Class 0-4-4T has just left the Esplanade station at Ryde and heads along the pier to take passengers to the paddle steamer, seen in the background, for the crossing to Portsmouth. JC

Right Standing at the beginning of the pier at Ryde is 'O2' No 31 *Chale*. This little engine dated back to April 1890 and was the second oldest on the island. It had been transferred from the mainland in May 1927 and was withdrawn in March 1967 when the lines were electrified. Conductor rails from Ryde Pier Head to Shanklin were energised on 1 March and the full electric service commenced from the 20th. JC

Above Class '02' No 21 *Sandown* stands light engine in Ryde Esplanade station. Note all the parcels and the platform clock. No 21 dated from September 1891 and had been transferred to the Isle of Wight in May 1924. Withdrawal came in May 1966. *JC*

Below Ventnor station, with '02' No 17 *Seaview* and St Boniface Down in the background. This engine transferred across in May 1930 and had previously been numbered 208. *JC*

Haven Street station, now the headquarters of the preserved Isle of Wight Steam Railway. Pushing through the rain is '02' No 16 *Ventnor*, with the fireman preparing to exchange the single-line tablet with the signalman. The engine had come over from the mainland in May 1936, its previous number being 217, and was withdrawn in December 1966. *JC*

The bridge arch at Wroxall station makes an excellent frame for 'O2' No 28 Ashey, which had joined the island's stock in March 1926. The train is from Ryde to Ventnor and the leading coach is an ex-London, Brighton & South Coast Railway vehicle. This section of line from Shanklin to Ventnor closed on 18 April 1966. JC

Above We move to Cowes in the driving rain for the final pair of photographs; '02' No 14 *Fishbourne* awaits departure with a train for Freshwater. This was the oldest locomotive on the island, being built at Nine Elms Works in December 1889 and previously numbered 178. It appeared on the island in May 1936 and lasted until December 1966. *JC*

Below Our last look at Isle of Wight steam on 21 August 1965 is '02' No 20 *Shanklin*, arriving at Cowes with a train from Freshwater. Note the pile of luggage on the station trolley, which will be loaded on to the train for the return journey. The Cowes to Newport branch closed to passengers on 21 February 1966, but remained open after this date for freight only to serve Medina Wharf where the conductor rails for the electrification were off-loaded after being conveyed from Redbridge by barge. *JC*

3. Steam at work: LMS

Left Liverpool Lime Street on Saturday 4 August 1962. With a good head of steam, Edge Hill-based rebuilt 'Patriot' 4-6-0 No 45535 *Sir Herbert Walker KCB* awaits departure for London in the early afternoon. This was the main afternoon departure for the capital and it was the usual practice to run a relief working 10 minutes or so before this departure, usually in the hands of a 'Pacific' locomotive. *JC*

Below The splendid arched roof of Lime Street station is shown to perfection in this scene recorded on Sunday 16 June 1963. Standing in the sunlight is red-liveried 'Princess Coronation' 4-6-2 No 46240 *City of Coventry* waiting time on a lightweight afternoon service to London. No 46240 remained in service until September 1964, when it retired from Crewe North shed. *JC*

Less majestic, but no less interesting, is 'Jinty' 0-6-0T No 47336 leaving Lime Street on empty stock for Downhill Carriage Sidings on 14 July 1962. Edge Hill maintained a batch of around 15 of these sturdy little engines, and they were a daily sight to add to the entertainment. This example dated from 1926 and had been built by the North British Locomotive Company. It lasted until June 1966, its last allocation being Lostock Hall. *JC*

Left Lime Street departure: 'Pacific' No 46245 *City of London* leaves with a relief working for London on Saturday 14 July 1962. This train was a regular working for one of these magnificent locomotives throughout 1962. The engine worked up on the Friday evening, was then serviced at Edge Hill shed, and returned south on this Saturday Only working. No 46245 was a Camden engine when this photograph was taken, and it formed part of the final allocation of four steam locomotives when the diesels took over at Camden eight weeks later on 9 September. Along with Nos 46239, 46240 and Ivatt 2-6-2T No 41239, it was sent to Willesden to work out its final service. No 46245 was transferred to Crewe North just before it was withdrawn in September 1964. *JC*

Below Lime Street arrival: on Saturday 2 September 1961 the 'Red Rose' completes its journey from London in the capable hands of Driver Donaghue and 'Princess Royal' Class 4-6-2 No 46207 *Princess Arthur of Connaught*, based at Camden. The engine was in fine form, for the arrival on this occasion was 25 minutes early. This may well have been No 46207's last appearance on this working, for the following week it was transferred to Willesden. Finding little work for the engine, it was withdrawn during the week-ended 2 December 1961. *JC*

Right Arriving at Lime Street at around 5.00 pm on Saturday 20 May 1961 is immaculate 'Patriot' 4-6-0 No 45547 with a working from Llandudno. This was a Llandudno Junction diagram and usually produced an equally clean Stanier '5MT' 4-6-0. The explanation for the appearance of the 'Patriot' was that during the following week it was transferred to Edge Hill shed and had been cleaned up for the run. It remained on Edge Hill's books until withdrawal in September 1962. JC

Below Reversing out of Lime Street after bringing in an earlier arrival is 'Princess Royal' 4-6-2 No 46209 *Princess Beatrice*. The engine will be serviced at Edge Hill during the day and take up its balanced working back to London on the following Sunday afternoon. The date of the photograph is Saturday 21 July 1962. No 46209 went into store at Camden two months later, on 10 September, and was withdrawn on 6 October. JC

Left The steep climb out from Lime Street continued through Edge Hill station and gave the photographer an ideal opportunity to catch the sight of steam locomotives working hard. This Sunday 21 February 1960 view has Crewe North-based 'Royal Scot' Class 4-6-0 No 46110 *Grenadier Guardsman* making the climb with the 10.30 am departure, which would end its journey at Plymouth. No 46110 had been rebuilt with a 2A boiler and double chimney in 1953 and was finally withdrawn during the week-ended 22 February 1964 from Carlisle Kingmoor. *PH*

Below The Victorian terraced houses look on at Edge Hill as ex-works Carlisle Upperby-based 'Princess Coronation' Class 4-6-2 No 46234 *Duchess of Abercorn* makes the climb look easy. It is again the 10.30 am Sunday working to Plymouth, the date this time being 17 April 1960. The locomotive would work as far as Shrewsbury and then be replaced by other power. No 46234 lasted in service until January 1963. *PH*

Storming up the incline alongside Edge Hill shed on its way to Wavertree Junction with the 10.05 am (Sunday) 'Merseyside Express' to Euston on 16 August 1959 is 'Princess Royal' 4-6-2 No 46211 *Queen Maud.* This was an Edge Hill engine at the time and looks to be steam-tight, but in filthy condition. Withdrawal for this locomotive came in October 1961. *PH*

Above As a result of an industrial dispute at Allerton depot, steam power returned to the Liverpool/Wigan locals in May 1966. On Monday 9 May Sutton Oak-allocated Ivatt 2MT 2-6-2T No 41286 passes Edge Hill shed on a train from St Helens. This little engine was built at Crewe Works and was run in from Crewe North during the week-ended 25 November 1950. It transferred to Sutton Oak shed (located at St Helens) during the week-ended 16 December 1950 and was still there when withdrawn in November 1966. *JC*

Below At the same location on Friday 2 April 1965, Stanier '8F' 2-8-0 No 48249 returns the Edge Hill breakdown train to its base after attending an incident. The scene is very different today, with the two near tracks lifted and the railway on the embankment removed. No 48249 had an interesting history, being built initially to a Ministry of Supply order during the Second World War and numbered 70314. It was later taken into British Railways stock and renumbered 48249, entering traffic during the week-ended 19 November 1949 at Crewe South shed. It was withdrawn in December 1966 from Edge Hill. *JC*

Storming past Edge Hill shed with a Liverpool to Newcastle train is 'Jubilee' 4-6-0 No 45590 *Travancore* on Monday 29 March 1965. The rostered Sulzer diesel had failed. This was the engine's first outing after having a complete re-tube of the boiler, which had been carried out at Edge Hill. This seems something of a waste of money and time as the engine was withdrawn later the same year in December from Warrington Dallam shed. It was eventually cut up at Cashmores, Great Bridge, in June 1966. *JC*

Climbing up to Wavertree and passing the backs of the terraced houses in Tiverton Street is filthy Stanier '5MT' 4-6-0 No 45312 on a London-bound working. It is a Sunday, the date being 12 September 1965, and the overhead equipment has been de-energised for cleaning, hence the steam traction. No 45312 dated back to February 1937 and was a product of the Armstrong Whitworth Company, going new to Willesden. It lasted into the last year of active steam working, being withdrawn from Bolton during the week-ended 29 June 1968. The 'going away' shot (*below*) shows the stiff gradient facing the engine. *JC*

Wavertree Junction on Saturday 3 October 1959. The freight lines to the famous 'Gridiron' sidings are on the left, now all gone. Rebuilt 'Patriot' 4-6-0 No 45527 *Southport*, Edge Hill-based, climbs powerfully away on the main line with the 4.00 pm to London. Edge Hill had two rebuilt 'Patriots' on its books at this time, the other being No 45531 *Sir Frederick Harrison*, along with three unrebuilt examples. No 45527 was withdrawn during the week-ended 5 December 1964 from Carlisle Kingmoor. *PH*

Left Wavertree station can be seen in the background of this scene recorded on Saturday 6 June 1959. Rather dirty rebuilt 'Patriot' 4-6-0 No 45535 *Sir Herbert Walker KCB* is in charge of the up 'Manxman'. Note the neat and tidy shrubs and box hedging to the left. Wavertree station closed on Tuesday 5 August 1958 after the North-West Transport Users Consultative Committee had agreed to this action. When this photograph was taken the station buildings were intact and used by railway staff. Today no trace of the station remains. No 45535 lasted until 1963, withdrawal coming from Carlisle Kingmoor during the week-ended 26 October. *PH*

Below The next station on the line out to Allerton and the West Coast Main Line was Sefton Park, which closed on Monday 2 May 1960. Stanier '5MT' 4-6-0 No 45410, another Edge Hill resident, passes by with a Liverpool to Birmingham express on Saturday 6 June 1959. No 45410 was withdrawn during the week-ended 10 September 1966 from Birmingham Saltley. *PH*

Our next location 3¾ miles out from Liverpool Lime Street is Mossley Hill, where a station is still open today. Following a visit to Crewe Works, clean ex-LNWR 'G2' 0-8-0 No 49404 has just passed the station with a freight bound for Edge Hill yards, including cows as passengers in the first wagon. The date is Wednesday 20 April 1960, and the masts for the electrification are appearing, spelling the end for scenes such as this. The electrified service from London Euston to Liverpool commenced on 18 April 1966, taking 155 minutes for the journey. Slow lumbering freights with elderly wheezing 'G2s' in charge did not fit into the scheme of things. No 49404 was withdrawn during the week-ended 28 April 1962 from Edge Hill and was in the cutting-up shop at Crewe on 20 May. PH

Proudly bearing 'The Merseyside Express' headboard, Edge Hill 'Royal Scot' 4-6-0 No 46156 *The South Wales Borderer* crosses the Mersey over Runcorn Bridge with the morning up working on a misty Saturday 9 May 1959. This was one of the 'Scots' that ended its service on the Great Central, withdrawal coming during the week-ended 10 October 1964 from Annesley. Runcorn Bridge was completed in 1868, opening for freight traffic on 1 February 1869 and for passengers in April. Its construction began in 1863 with the excavations for the foundations of the four sand-stone piers to carry the lattice-girder spans. During the digging remains were found that were associated with Runcorn Castle and Ethelfleda, King Alfred's daughter; hence the bridge's local name, the 'Ethelfleda'. The River Mersey at this point is 1,000 feet wide, and the deck of the bridge had to be 75 feet above high water level to give adequate clearance to ships passing underneath. *PH*

Above We return to Liverpool Lime Street for this view of Edge Hill Stanier '5MT' 4-6-0 No 45305 awaiting departure with the Locomotive Club of Great Britain 'Lancastrian' tour on Saturday 6 April 1968. The train ran via Warrington Arpley to Stockport, then via Manchester Piccadilly and Ordsall Lane to Eccles, returning to Liverpool Lime Street via Tyldesley, Springs Branch, Wigan Wallgate, Southport St Lukes and Liverpool Riverside. No 45305 transferred to Lostock Hall shortly after, when Edge Hill shed closed, and remained active until the end of steam. It was in steam on the last day, Sunday 4 August, and worked an enthusiasts' special. It is now preserved and named *Alderman A. E. Draper*. JC

Right Later in the tour, on its last few miles, No 45305 is seen leaving Riverside station, Pier Head, Liverpool, and passing the well-known landmarks on the waterfront. The Liver Building in the background contains the clock known as the 'Great George', which was set in motion on 23 June 1911 at the precise moment that King George V was being crowned in Westminster Abbey. JC

Left Liverpool Sandhills station on the third-rail electrified line out to Southport. The date is Friday 7 July 1967 and Stanier '5MT' 4-6-0 No 45376 is Blackpool-bound with one of three specials run by the Littlewoods catalogue and pools company for their employees annual day out. The large building in the background is the ex-Midland Railway warehouse at Sandon Dock, which was demolished in 1971. No 45376 was another survivor into 1968, going in March from Edge Hill. *JC*

Below City-bound commuters watch a scene that in a few more months will be history. The setting is Orrell Park station 4 miles out from Liverpool City Centre in March 1968. The 9.00 am Liverpool Exchange to Glasgow train hurries by in the capable hands of Stanier '5MT' 4-6-0 No 44851, withdrawn a few weeks later when allocated to Manchester Newton Heath. Orrell Park is still open, serving the Liverpool Central to Ormskirk Merseyrail electric services. *JC*

The annual Grand National Race at Aintree was over on Saturday 27 March 1965 and a returning special is seen at Stanley on the Bootle branch. The engines are clean Stanier '5MT' 4-6-0 No 45070, allocated to Wigan Springs Branch, and 'Britannia' 4-6-2 No 70052 *Firth of Tay* from Crewe North. The first to be withdrawn was the 'Britannia' during the week-ended 1 April 1967 from Carlisle Kingmoor. No 45070 lasted a little longer, Warrington Dallam losing its services during the week-ended 20 May of the same year. *JC*

Above Walton Junction, on the line from Liverpool Exchange, on a cloudy Saturday 15 August 1964. Passing the signal box is the afternoon train to Glasgow with rebuilt 'Patriot' 4-6-0 No 45512 *Bunsen* in charge. Active members of this Class on passenger workings were rare by this time, and *Bunsen* was one of the last three to remain in service, withdrawal coming from Carlisle Kingmoor during the week-ended 27 March 1965. *JC*

Below Stanier '4MT' 2-6-4T No 42655 makes an impressive sight passing Kirkby station signal box on a lengthy eight-coach local working to Wigan Wallgate from Liverpool Exchange on Saturday 31 January 1959. No 42655 had been built in 1941 at Derby Works and spent its British Railways career working from Bolton shed, from where it was withdrawn during the week-ended 12 January 1963. It remained in store at Bolton until April, then moved to Horwich Works for cutting up. *PH*

The dying days of steam traction in Lancashire. The date is a damp Tuesday 16 July 1968, with only three weeks left until the final steam workings. The location is Rose Grove West signal box and Stanier '8F' 2-8-0 No 48775 is held at signals on a mixed goods. The engine was taken into stock in September 1957 along with two others, Nos 48773 and 48774, from the War Department. They were sent to Glasgow Polmadie and were the only examples of this type allocated to the Scottish Region; Carlisle Kingmoor was the nearest depot that had any on allocation at the time. All three eventually came south, after temporary withdrawal, to English sheds, and were distinctive by having modified top-feeds. No 48773 is preserved, but No 48775 was withdrawn at the very end of steam and went for scrap. JC

Above With steam being ejected through open cylinder drain cocks, Stanier '8F' 2-8-0 No 48348 climbs out of Rose Grove on a goods and mineral train in March 1968. This engine had first entered traffic in April 1944 at Nottingham. Withdrawal took place from Rose Grove during the last week of steam working. *JC*

Left Our look at LMS steam now moves to the West Coast Main Line, and we follow the line to Carlisle, starting at Crewe on Sunday 12 July 1964 with the Stephenson Locomotive Society special train 1X82, 'The Pennine Three Summits' railtour. This train left Birmingham New Street at 8.51 am, 1 minute late, with 11 coaches, 600 passengers, and in charge Stanier 'Pacific' No 46251 *City of Nottingham*, which took the train over Shap summit to Carlisle. From Carlisle the special changed engines to another member of the class, No 46255 *City of Hereford*, for a run over Ais Gill summit to Leeds. Here, 'Jubilee' 4-6-0 No 45647 *Sturdee* took over for the route over Standedge summit, through Huddersfield, Marsden, Stalybridge, Guide Bridge, Heaton Norris and Crewe, which was reached 4½ minutes early. From Crewe 'Royal Scot' 4-6-0 No 46155 *The Lancer* returned the train to Birmingham. The whole tour cost 45 shillings (£2.25) for the 450 miles behind steam. This photograph shows Leeds Holbeck-based No 45647 just after arrival at Crewe. *JC*

Above 'Royal Scot' No 46155 has now come on to special 1X82 and prepares to leave Crewe for Birmingham. *JC*

Below A few moments later No 46155 gets away with an explosive exhaust and the crew keeping a wary eye on things. From 1 September 1964

'Jubilees', 'Royal Scots' and Stanier 'Pacifics' were barred from working south from Crewe as the height of the electric wires was lower than was the case northwards. No 46155 was kept in good condition for working rail-tours but was finally withdrawn during the week-ended 12 December 1964 from Carlisle Kingmoor. *JC*

Above Acton Grange Junction, south of Warrington, on Saturday 17 August 1963. The last Stanier basic-design Class '5MT' 4-6-0 to be built, No 44687, allocated to Llandudno Junction, comes off the line from Chester with a Llandudno to Manchester express working; its next stop will be Warrington Bank Quay. This locomotive was a hybrid of the Class '5' and was fitted with Caprotti valve gear, Skefko roller bearings and a high running-plate. Only two were so built, the other being No 44686, and they were the forerunners of the Standard-type '5MT' 4-6-0s built by British Railways. No 44687, built at Horwich, entered traffic during the week-ended 26 May 1951 and operated from Manchester Longsight until September 1960 when it transferred to Crewe South. The following month Llandudno Junction received the loco, where it joined sister engine No 44686. Both moved on to Southport in October 1963, where they remained until withdrawal, No 44686 going during the week-ended 16 October 1965 and No 44687 the week-ended 22 January 1966. *PH*

Left A very cold night at Warrington on Friday 13 January 1967 finds Stanier '8F' 2-8-0 No 48437 from Stockport Edgeley shed and an unidentified Standard '9F' 2-10-0 held at signals. The 2-8-0 is equipped with a snow plough in preparation for bad weather. No 48437 was a product of Swindon Works in May 1944 and was first allocated to the GWR shed at Chester. It was another survivor into the last year of steam, going during the week-ended 30 March, still at Stockport. *JC*

Right The next sequence of photographs were taken on Saturday 23 April 1960 at Boars Head, a few miles north of Wigan. Recent track re-laying is in evidence as rebuilt 'Jubilee' 4-6-0 No 45735 *Comet* heads north, climbing the 1 in 104 bank. A station was provided at Boars Head, but was closed on 31 January 1949. *Comet* had been rebuilt in 1942 with a 2A-type boiler and double chimney, and finished working during the week-ended 3 October 1964 from Annesley on the Great Central. It remained at Crewe Works until December, then went for breaking up at Cashmores, Great Bridge. *PH*

Below Drifting down Boars Head Bank, but still making plenty of smoke, is 'Patriot' 4-6-0 No 45542, bearing a 24K Preston shedplate. This is a Barrow to Euston express, and the first coach, which is an ex-LMS vehicle, was a through working from Workington. No 45542 had the name *Dunoon* selected for it, but the naming was never carried out. The engine was withdrawn during the week-ended 9 June 1962 from Nuneaton shed. *PH*

Above The stirring sight of a 'Duchess': 'Pacific' No 46234 *Duchess of Abercorn*, in British Railways standard green livery, rolls down Boars Head with a Glasgow to Birmingham express. Having entered traffic in August 1938, by 1960 No 46234 had clocked up a mileage of over one and a half million. *PH*

Below A northbound parcels working, with an interesting selection of vans, is hauled up Boars Head by 'Jubilee' 4-6-0 No 45634 *Trinidad*, based at Crewe North. In November 1960 the engine transferred to Willesden for a year, then returned to Crewe, this time to South shed. There it remained until withdrawal during the week-ended 11 May 1963. Cutting up took place at Crewe Works in August. *PH*

Right Six years later at Boars Head, in March 1966, Carlisle Kingmoor Stanier '5MT' 4-6-0 No 44878 drifts down the bank with a lengthy up freight and nears the outskirts of Wigan. No 44878 went new to Kingmoor from Crewe Works in May 1945 and remained there until the depot closed to steam on 31 December 1967. It then transferred to Lostock Hall where it remained until withdrawal during the week-ended 6 July 1968. *JC*

Below We now move further north to near Farington Junction, south of Preston, in July 1962. A southbound express composed of ex-LMS coaches is hauled by one of only five named Stanier '5MT' 4-6-0s, No 45154 *Lanarkshire Yeomanry*. The locomotive was built by Armstrong Whitworth in June 1935 and first operated from Crewe North. Naming took place in 1937 when the engine was allocated to Scotland. Spending many years at Glasgow St Rollox shed, it returned to England in April 1957 to Manchester Newton Heath, displaced from Glasgow by the new Caprotti-fitted Standard '5MT' 4-6-0s. Withdrawal came during the week-ended 12 November 1966 from Speke Junction. *PH*

Above Preston station on Monday 6 August 1962, looking rather untidy with litter lying amongst the track. Also looking uncared for is 'Jubilee' 4-6-0 No 45552 *Silver Jubilee* on an express working. This locomotive started as No 5642, but swapped identity with the original No 5552 in April 1935. This enabled the newer engine to be specially painted in black livery with a chrome-plated 'silver lining' effect as the LMS celebrated the Silver Jubilee of King George V and Queen Mary. It also had raised silver-plated numbers on the cab sides, which it retained until withdrawal from Crewe North during the week-ended 26 September 1964. *JC*

Left On the same day 'Royal Scot' 4-6-0 No 46132 *The Kings Regiment Liverpool* makes a lot of noise at Preston with its safety valves roaring away awaiting departure with an express. No 46132 was withdrawn from Carlisle Kingmoor during the week-ended 1 February 1964. *JC*

A view in the Lune Valley as Edge Hill-allocated 'Princess Royal' 'Pacific' No 46204 Princess Louise heads north with the 'Royal Scot' on Monday 14 September 1959, picking up water on Dillicar troughs. This was a gruelling trip for footplate crews and the tender already looks half empty. Both driver and fireman are taking a breather after the climb over Grayrigg summit, and are enjoying the fresh air and the scenery on the 5½ miles of level and slightly favourable road before the ascent of Shap. *PH*

Left Penrith station on a very cold Saturday 2 April 1966. Ivatt '2MT' 2-6-0s Nos 46458 and 46426 have just changed places with LNER preserved 'Pacific' No 4472 *Flying Scotsman* for a run over the Keswick branch and on to Workington and Arnside. The joint SLS/MLS 'Lakes & Fells' tour had started from Manchester Exchange at 9.05 am and ran via Wigan, Leyland, Bamber Bridge and Blackburn to Hellifield powered by 'Jubilee' No 45596 *Bahamas*. Here *Flying Scotsman* took over to Penrith, going via Appleby and Carlisle Upperby. No 4472 took over again at Arnside for the return to Hellifield, then No 45596 took the train back to Manchester - all this for 57s 6d (£2.87). The two Ivatt 2-6-0s were allocated to Workington at the time and both were withdrawn later in the year, No 46426 during the week-ended 24 September and No 46458 the week-ended 17 December. *JC*

Below Carlisle Citadel station, south end, in February 1965. Stanier '5MT' 4-6-0 No 44887, Kingmoor-allocated, makes a start on a southbound extra. Hiding in the background is an Ivatt 2-6-2T on station pilot duties. An overall roof once covered this part of the station, but this was removed in 1957, the retaining wall in the background originally forming the support. *JC*

Above Not the 'Royal Scot', but just as important was the London-bound milk train. Speed was essential to get this train to the dairies in time for Londoners' breakfasts the next day. On Sundays it was worked as a separate train leaving Carlisle at around 4.00 pm; on other days the milk wagons were attached to the rear of an up express. This is a Sunday scene, on 29 July 1962, and the locomotive is Polmadie-based 'Princess Coronation' 4-6-2 No 46221 *Queen Elizabeth*, waiting a change of crew. *JC*

Right The second rebuilt 'Jubilee' 4-6-0, No 45736 *Phoenix*, stands awaiting an engine change at the south end of Carlisle station on Saturday 18 July 1964. It was withdrawn the following month from Carlisle Kingmoor and placed in store there until December when it was sold for scrap. *JC*

Above The north end of Carlisle station on Monday 7 August 1961. Kingmoor's 'Princess Coronation' 4-6-2 No 46252 *City of Leicester* has replaced another engine and is anxious to be away with an afternoon London to Perth express. Built at Crewe in June 1944, No 46252 was first allocated to Crewe North and remained there for many years. Carlisle Upperby also had use of the locomotive, but its final home was Camden, withdrawal coming during the week-ended 1 June 1963, with a registered mileage of 1,231,032. It had been stored since August 1962 alongside the Camden coaling plant, and left for scrapping at Crewe Works when the shed closed to steam in September 1963. *PH*

Below On 2 September 1962 'Princess Coronation' 4-6-2 No 46257 *City of Salford* is seen taking water after working in from Liverpool Exchange on the early Sunday morning train for Glasgow, which had become a regular duty for this type of locomotive. No 46257 was the last of the Class to be built in June 1948, and was withdrawn during the week-ended 12 September 1964 from Kingmoor. *JC*

Standing at the same spot on Saturday 13 February 1965 is the last active 'Royal Scot', 4-6-0 No 46115 *Scots Guardsman*. It is heading the RCTS 'The Rebuilt Scot Commemorative Tour', which should have been hauled by sister engine No 46160 *Queen Victoria's Rifleman*, but this failed with a hot axle the previous week. No 46115 was therefore transformed from a grubby nameless 'Scot' to a very presentable appearance with replacement nameplates, made of plywood, at Crewe North during the week before the tour. Manned by Driver Fisher and his mate from Crewe North throughout, the ten-coach 380-ton train, with 450 passengers, started from Crewe

and ran through to Boars Head. Here it took the line through Chorley, Blackburn and Hellifield for a run over the Settle & Carlisle, the engine having a particularly pronounced knock from the motion echoing away through the cuttings. At Carlisle there was an hour and a half break for the locomotive to be serviced, and our photograph shows it just before it set off to Kingmoor light engine. A return to Crewe down the West Coast Main Line then took place. No 46115 was withdrawn later in the year during the week-ended 31 December from Kingmoor, but is still with us in preservation. JC

Above We now move into Scotland, with this view at Paisley station on a sunny day in July 1965. At the head of a mixed freight, Glasgow Corkerhill-allocated Stanier '5MT' 4-6-0 No 44798, with its top feed cover missing, lets off steam through the safety valves. No 44798 was a relatively new engine, having been built at Horwich Works in October 1947. It was allocated new to Inverness where it remained until the Highland lines were dieselised in the early 1960s. It spent its entire working life in Scotland and was withdrawn on 2 September 1966, still at Corkerhill. *JC*

Left Ayr was the last shed in Scotland to operate the Hughes/Fowler 'Crab' 2-6-0s, and this July 1965 photograph has No 42919 sooting up Ayr station roof on a heavy train of coal wagons. This example was Crewe built in November 1930 and spent its British Railways career operating from sheds in the south-west of Scotland. *JC*

Stirling station in August 1965, with Stanier '5MT' 4-6-0 No 44992 quite a long way from its home base at Hurlford. The driver keeps his eye on the tank water gauge to save spillage as the engine takes water before leaving on a freight working. No 44992 was another locomotive to go new to Inverness, this time in January 1947, from Horwich. Withdrawal from Hurlford came about on 31 December 1966. JC

Above An interior view of Edinburgh Princes Street, the former Caledonian Railway station, on Friday 17 July 1964, with Fairburn '4MT' 2-6-4T No 42058 ready to return home to Carstairs. The engine carries a 66E Carstairs shedplate, but still has its former shed Polmadie painted in full on the buffer beam. This engine had moved to Carstairs the previous May, its first transfer since going new from Derby Works to Polmadie in November 1950. It remained at Carstairs until withdrawn on 24 August 1966. Princes Street was closed completely at midnight on Saturday 4 September 1965. The last two departures were both steam worked by Carstairs '5MT' 4-6-0s, the Saturday Only 10.30 pm to Lanark by No 45171 and the 11.30 pm to Birmingham and Liverpool by No 44954. *JC*

Left We return to England and the Wirral for this view at Birkenhead Woodside station. Stanier '4MT' 2-6-4T No 42616, with red-backed numberplate, is employed on station pilot duties on Sunday 5 March 1967, the last day of through passenger services to Paddington (see the photograph of No 7029 on page 22). The last departure for Paddington left at 9.40 pm behind Stanier '5MT' 4-6-0 No 44690, leaving 5 minutes late accompanied by the sound of exploding detonators. No 42616 transferred from Birkenhead to Bradford Low Moor on 29 April and was finally withdrawn on 30 September 1967. Birkenhead Woodside closed on 5 November 1967. *JC*

Right Chester is our next location, near Roodee Junction, the photographs being taken from the City Walls where they bridge the railway. Bangor-based Stanier '5MT' 4-6-0 No 45225 leaves the city on a Saturday special for North Wales on 22 April 1961. Over to the right is the Shropshire Union Canal, which at this point descends a flight of locks to go under the railway and eventually join the River Dee. No 45225 moved on to Stockport Edgeley, from where it was withdrawn during the week-ended 14 October 1967. *PH*

Below The same spot on Monday 8 May 1961 finds LMS 'Jinty' '3F' 0-6-0T No 47371, in very clean condition, trundling past with a transfer freight out to the yards at Mold Junction. This engine dated from 1926 and had been built by the North British Locomotive Company. It was allocated to Mold Junction from 1948 to December 1958, then moved to Chester LMS shed, from where it was withdrawn during the week-ended 2 October 1965. *PH*

Above Another photograph recorded on 8 May 1961. Ex-works Stanier '5MT' 4-6-0 No 44892, a Carnforth engine, makes an eye-catching sight as it backs down to Chester General station. The line through Chester was no stranger to engines fresh off Crewe Works, being used as a running-in ground, as it still is today. No 44892 first took to the rails in September 1945 at Manchester Newton Heath and worked from a number of North West sheds, including Carlisle Canal. It settled at Carnforth in June 1951, where it remained until withdrawal during the week-ended 8 August 1967. *PH*

Below left A nostalgic and rather sad photograph of the last Hughes/Fowler 'Crab' 2-6-0 to remain active, No 42942, with 'LMS' uncovered on the tender. The date is Bank Holiday Monday, 29 August 1966, and the location Llandudno station, with the engine waiting to return home with its train of daytrippers. This was regarded as the last appearance of a 'Crab' on a public long-distance train, which was a packed excursion from Rock Ferry loaded to ten corridor coaches. Although a heavy train, No 42942 attained maximum speeds of 64 mph at Mollington and 65 mph at Holywell Junction on the outward journey, with 69 mph at Holywell on the return. The 23 miles from Prestatyn to Mold Junction were covered in 26 minutes, with speed being maintained in the 60s for 15 miles. All this was under the capable control of Driver F. Part and Fireman A. Turner on the outward run, and Driver B. Williams and Fireman N. Warburton on the return, all based at Birkenhead, as was the engine. The 'Crab' had been smartened up the previous day by a band of enthusiasts working at the shed with paint and paraffin. They then enjoyed the trip on the Monday armed with cameras and tape recorders, taking over the front coach. The long reign of the 'Crabs' came to an end on Saturday 14 January 1967 when No 42942 worked the 5.40 am Bidston Yard to Dee Marsh pick-up freight. It was officially withdrawn the next week and remained at Birkenhead shed awaiting disposal along with the other survivors, Nos 42727, 42765, 42782 and 42859. A bid to save the engine for preservation failed when insufficient money was raised by the time the British Railways deadline arrived. It remained stored at Birkenhead until October, when it was towed away for scrap. Three of the class still survive, Nos 42700, 42765 and 42859, secured for future generation to enjoy. *JC*

4. Steam at work: LNER

Right We commence our look at ex-LNER locomotives at Edinburgh Waverley on Saturday 2 June 1962. The famous King's Cross-based Gresley 'A4' 4-6-2 No 60022 *Mallard* is about to come off train 1F78 and be replaced by Haymarket's sister engine No 60004 *William Whitelaw*. This was during the working of the special 'Aberdeen Flyer', which was intended to be the last non-stop steam-worked run from King's Cross to Edinburgh. The train left King's Cross promptly at 8.00 am with No 60022 in charge of the eight coaches for the 393 miles to Edinburgh, the time allowed being 6 hours 25 minutes. All went well with time kept until the train was forced to a stand at Chathill, just south of Berwick, due to a wagon in a goods train ahead developing a hot axle. This spoiled an otherwise excellent run, and arrival was only 20 minutes late at Edinburgh. The tour participants were not too disappointed as they had enjoyed a sumptuous breakfast on the train, an attractive commemorative menu card and route itinerary, as well as a special 'Aberdeen Flyer Cocktail'. One notable passenger was Peter Handford, who recorded for Argo the sounds of the 'Pacific' from the front guards van. As seen here, No 60004 came on at Edinburgh to cover the 130 miles to Aberdeen with seven coaches (the Kitchen car was removed at Edinburgh), arriving at 6.03 pm. *JC*

Below Another view at Waverley station, this time in August 1965. Gresley 'V2' 2-6-2 No 60813, St Margarets-allocated, awaits departure with a train for Perth, and is unique in being fitted with mini-smoke-deflectors and stovepipe chimney. These were fitted in 1947 to cure the problem of drifting smoke, but did somewhat spoil the good looks of the engine. No 60813 was put to traffic at Doncaster shed on 27 September 1937 as LNER No 4784. It survived a visit to Darlington Works in August 1963 and lasted in service until 26 September 1966. *JC*

Above This is Stonehaven in early August 1965, with 'A4' 4-6-2 No 60006 *Sir Ralph Wedgwood* operating one of the 3-hour Aberdeen to Glasgow expresses. This was the swansong of the 'A4s' and received a great deal of attention from railway enthusiasts, being the last opportunity to see these engines in action on express workings. No 60006 did not last much longer, for withdrawal came on 3 September from Aberdeen Ferryhill after being out of service from mid-August following its failure. *JC*

Below Another view at Stonehaven on the same day. This time the locomotive is 'A4' 4-6-2 No 60034 *Lord Faringdon* on a Glasgow to Aberdeen service. No 60034 lasted into 1966, being withdrawn on 24 August. The reign of the 'A4s' came to an end at Ferryhill shortly afterwards with the withdrawal of the final two, Nos 60019 *Bittern* and 60024 *Kingfisher* on 5 September. *JC*

Above Class 'J37' '5F' 0-6-0 No 64571 is at Inverkeithing on a freight, possibly from Rosyth Dockyard, with some interesting contents in the wagons. The date is Tuesday 6 July 1965. Inverkeithing, on the north side of the Forth Bridge, was the junction for the Naval Dockyard branch as well as those to Dunfermline and Kirkcaldy, and remains open today served by the Outer Circle workings from Edinburgh. The 'J37' Class locomotives were a Reid design for the North British dating from 1914, and all were allocated to Scotland. No 64571 spent most of its British Railways days allocated to Polmont shed before moving to Grangemouth in May 1964 and Dunfermline in October of the same year, from where it was withdrawn on 23 October 1965. It was cut up in January 1966 at Arnott Youngs yard at Carmyle. *JC*

Below Another 'J37' 0-6-0, this time No 64636 engaged in some shunting at Larbert on the Glasgow to Stirling line. The date is Saturday 18 May 1963 and this was another long-time member of the Polmont allocation. Also moving to Grangemouth in May 1964 when Polmont shed closed, it remained there until withdrawal on 12 October of the same year. After storage it was cut up at Motherwell Machinery and Scrap Co at Wishaw in January 1965. *JC*

Carlisle Citadel station again, on Monday 7 August 1961. 'A3' 4-6-2 No 60099 *Call Boy* stands at the south end of the station after arriving from Edinburgh via the Waverley route; it will next go to Carlisle Canal shed for servicing. *Call Boy* was built at Doncaster in April 1930 and numbered LNER No 2795. It acquired the number 99 in July 1946 and 60099 in July 1949. The double chimney was added in July 1958, and the German-type smoke-deflectors only a month before this photograph was taken. Withdrawal from Edinburgh St Margarets shed was actioned on 28 October 1963. *PH*

Above We now move to York station on Saturday 15 July 1961, and find 'A1' 4-6-2 No 60138 *Boswell* leaving on an express for Newcastle. These Peppercorn-designed locomotives were the last 'Pacifics' to be built to an LNER design, and all took to the rails after nationalisation. Peppercorn's predecessor, Edward Thompson, had injected many ideas into the design and these were perpetuated after he had retired. No 60138 entered service in December 1948, being built at Darlington, and went new to York where it remained all its working life until withdrawal on 4 October 1965. It will be interesting soon to see a new member of the Class, currently under construction and to be numbered 60163. *JC*

Right Compare the 'A1' to this example of the Peppercorn 'A2' Class 4-6-2, No 60539 *Bronzino*. This was the last one to be built, in August 1948. The date of this photograph is Saturday 23 July 1960 and the location Leeds City station. Heaton depot had the pleasure of this locomotive when new, and there it remained until 1961, Tweedmouth then acquiring it, from where it was withdrawn on 12 November 1962. *JC*

Left The Gresley-designed 'J50' Class 0-6-0T was a useful and reliable locomotive and was scattered all over the old Great Northern Railway area. There was also a batch of seven (68952 to 68958) allocated to Glasgow Eastfield in the 1950s. This view, taken from a train awaiting entry to Leeds Central station in August 1962, shows No 68984 moving empty stock to Copley Hill carriage sidings. Copley Hill engine shed maintained around six of these engines, but by the end of 1962 only 12 remained active out of an original class total of 102, all being withdrawn by 23 September 1963. No 68984 was withdrawn on 25 March during the Class's last year. Leeds Central station closed on 29 April 1967 and it was reported that an audience of over 1,000 people, thronged on platform ends, at the lineside and in the signal box, witnessed the last rites. The final movement was Holbeck's Ivatt 2-6-2T No 41245 clearing the remaining vans in the evening. *JC*

Above right London Liverpool Street station on Saturday 26 April 1958 - 'B2' Class 4-6-0 No 61671 *Royal Sovereign*, down from Cambridge, is being turned in readiness for the return journey. This locomotive was kept in very good condition for use on Royal Train duties. The 'B2' was a derivative of the Gresley 'B17' 4-6-0, being fitted with the 'B1'-type 100A boiler by Edward Thompson in an attempt to improve performance. Both types had a reputation for being rough riders, particularly when nearing the time for works attention. No 61671 spent its British Railways days allocated to Cambridge and was withdrawn on 22 September 1958. *JC*

Below Compare the Thompson 'B1' to the 'B2' in the previous photograph. We cross London to King's Cross station for this August 1962 view of 'B1' 4-6-0 No 61168 entering on an express from Cleethorpes. This was a working for Immingham-based members of the Class, and this example dated from June 1947, first operating from Gorton. After a spell at Mexborough, Immingham became the engine's home and it remained there until withdrawal on 3 October 1965. *JC*

Left Two views of 'A4' 4-6-2 No 60034 *Lord Faringdon* before the engine was transferred to Scotland. The date is Sunday 12 August 1962 and the location is Doncaster, with the 'Pacific' heading south. *JC*

Below The second photograph is again in August 1962, with *Lord Faringdon* this time getting to grips with a northbound express at King's Cross. *JC*

5. Steam at work: BR Standards

We return to Carlisle Citadel station in February 1965 for this view of nameless 'Britannia' 4-6-2 No 70001 making itself heard with the safety valves blowing. This is the north end of the station and the formerly named *Lord Hurcomb* is awaiting an arrival from the south for an engine change. Allocated new to Stratford depot from Crewe Works on 14 February 1951, the engine served from Norwich and March before transfer to the LMR at Willesden in March 1963. A brief period at Aston later in 1963 was followed by transfer to Carlisle Kingmoor in October 1964, from where withdrawal took place during the week-ended 3 September 1966. *JC*

The last survivor of the 'Britannias' was No 70013 *Oliver Cromwell*, which is now confined to Bressingham Museum in Norfolk amid controversy as to its being allowed to run again on British Rail. One of the engine's last runs on the main line is recorded here on Sunday 21 July 1968 at Southport Chapel Street. This was part of a railtour that had made two return trips from Manchester. It ran west from Manchester Victoria behind Stanier 4-6-0 No 44888 via Newton-le-Willows, Edge Lane and Bootle, returning with *Oliver Cromwell* on the L&Y route via Wigan and Bolton. The 'Britannia' then continued on the next stage to Southport via Rochdale, Todmorden, Rose Grove and Burscough Bridge. Another Stanier 4-6-0, No 45110, returned the train to Manchester Central via Burscough, Aintree Central, Hough Green and Warrington Central. *JC*

Above 'Britannia' 4-6-2 No 70018, formerly *Flying Dutchman*, passes Edge Hill shed watched by members of the shed staff on the foggy, frosty morning of Tuesday 28 December 1965. Steam traction on main-line passenger work was becoming increasingly rare and this working was due to the rostered diesel not being available. No 70018 was at this date a Crewe South engine, but evidence of its earlier days on the Western Region are borne out by the smoke deflectors not having hand rails, but grab-holes instead. *Flying Dutchman* had first operated from Old Oak Common on 30 June 1951, but ex-GWR men did not get on well with their new locomotives, one complaint being poor visibility. As a result of the derailment of No 70026 at New Milton between Steventon and Didcot on 20 November 1955, partly blamed on obscured visibility, the handrails were removed from the deflectors on Western Region-allocated locomotives. Some of the best work on the Western was obtained when all the 'Britannias' on the Region were concentrated at Cardiff Canton. Eventually all moved to the LMR on 11 September 1961. No 70018 went to Carlisle Canal and later moved on to Kingmoor, after its time at Crewe. It was withdrawn during the week-ended 24 December 1966. *JC*

Left Another 'Britannia' deputising for a failed diesel and also allocated to Crewe South. It is June 1965 and No 70052, once named *Firth Of Tay*, passes Edge Hill station on a Newcastle train. This example had been delivered new to Glasgow Polmadie in August 1954, and by March 1962 it had crossed the city to be allocated to Corkerhill. Then followed time at Crewe North, Crewe South, Banbury, and, in January 1966, Kingmoor from where it was withdrawn at the end of March 1967. *JC*

Only ten 'Clan' 4-6-2s were built, divided between Glasgow Polmadie and Carlisle Kingmoor. All the Scottish-based examples, including No 72003 *Clan Fraser* seen in this photograph, were withdrawn on 29 December 1962, but the Carlisle batch went during 1965 and 1966. This view is at the south end of Carlisle Citadel station on a dull afternoon in August 1961. The train is a Glasgow to Liverpool and Manchester service, on which the 'Clans' were regular performers. Note that No 72003 still carries the earlier British Railways totem on the tender, which had been discontinued from 1957. *PH*

Left The unique 'Pacific' No 71000 *Duke of Gloucester*, now thankfully preserved. This is a photograph taken on Saturday 25 August 1962 and 'The Duke' has just arrived at Liverpool Lime Street with the 'Red Rose' from London. It had only three months of active life left after this, for withdrawal took place during the week-ended 24 November. *JC*

Below We return to Birkenhead Woodside again on Sunday 5 March 1967 and find a very dirty Manchester Patricroft Standard '5MT' 4-6-0, No 73139, on a last-day Birkenhead to Paddington through working. No 73139 was one of 30 members of the Class to be fitted with Caprotti valve gear; built at Derby, it entered traffic at Holyhead during the week-ended 24 November 1956. It moved on to Leicester Midland and in January 1959 to its birthplace, Derby. From November 1959 it moved with nine others to Rowsley in the Peak District, then to Patricroft in June 1964. Withdrawal came during the week-ended 13 May 1967. *JC*

Above Another batch of the Caprotti-fitted Standard '5MT' 4-6-0s, Nos 73145 to 73154 inclusive, all went to Scotland in 1957 and were allocated new to Glasgow St Rollox. They remained in Scotland for all their short working lives and were a familiar sight working out from Glasgow Buchanan Street station, which is where we see this example, No 73153, reversing out on empty stock in June 1965. The engine remained at St Rollox until 7 November 1966, when the shed closed, then transferred to Stirling, from where it was withdrawn the next month on the 10th. Glasgow Buchanan Street station also closed on 7 November 1966. *JC*

Right Conventional Standard '5MT' 4-6-0 No 73165 is caught by the camera on Sunday 21 February 1960 on the 11.00 am Liverpool to Leeds train approaching Roby station. The engine was a Leeds Holbeck-maintained machine and looks in fine form with a clean exhaust and no steam leaks. This was another of the Class that ended its days at Patricroft, going during the week-ended 2 October 1965. *PH*

Above Two views of Standard '5MT' 4-6-0 No 73169 at Bournemouth Central on Monday 5 September 1966, less than a year before steam on the Southern finished. The first view shows the engine passing the engine shed yard and approaching the station on a London-bound train. *JC*

Below No 73169 gets the road and prepares to leave the station, next stop Southampton. No 73169 was a late arrival on the Southern, being received at Feltham in September 1963. Before that it had been delivered to York shed from Doncaster Works in April 1957, then spent time at Leeds Holbeck, Scarborough, Neville Hill and Wakefield. From Feltham it moved to Eastleigh in November 1964, and was withdrawn in October 1966. *JC*

Above It is to York that we now go, to find one of the rarer British Railways Standard types, the Class '3MT' 2-6-0. Here No 77012 enters York station on Saturday 13 July 1963 with a passenger train from the Scarborough line. A Class of only 20 engines, all worked in the North East and Scotland, but towards the end of steam operation two went to Northwich, Nos 77011 and 77014, and this last one eventually got as far south as Guildford. The Class was constructed at Swindon Works, and No

77012 went first to Darlington shed in June 1954 and later transferred to York, where it remained until September 1963. It then started to wander: Leeds Stourton, Farnley Junction, Bradford Manningham, Hull Dairycoates, Goole, and South Blyth all had its services until, like the proverbial bad penny, it returned to York in April 1966 until withdrawal on 12 June 1967. JC

Below The popular and well-designed Standard '4MT' 2-6-4T is seen next in the shape of No 80086. The location is Wemyss Bay, and the train has just arrived from Glasgow on a sunny day in July 1965. Bury was the first home for this engine in June 1954 before it moved on to Manchester Newton Heath in July 1956, then to Chester in October of the same year. Scotland claimed the engine in April 1960 when it went to Edinburgh Dalry Road, then Carstairs, and finally Glasgow Polmadie in November 1960. Here it remained until withdrawn on 1 May 1967. JC

Looking somewhat out of place on a freight working is Standard '4MT' 2-6-4T No 80098. Even the location is not one associated with the Class, for it is at the top of Talerddig Bank on the Cambrian line. The date is Friday 2 August 1963 and the freight is on its way to Shrewsbury. This engine was more associated with the London, Tilbury & Southend line from Fenchurch Street. It went brand new to Plaistow from Brighton Works in December 1954, and moved on to Tilbury in November 1959. When the line was electrified in 1962 it was made redundant, but instead of going for scrap it found a new life on the Western Region. A 'paper only' transfer to Old Oak Common in August 1962 got it away from the Eastern Region, then on to Shrewsbury the next month. After a brief interlude at Wrexham Croes Newydd, it settled down at Machynlleth in March 1963, turning a final wheel in revenue-earning service in July 1965. *PH*

Above Love them or hate them, the WD 'Austerity' '8F' 2-8-0s were very much part of the railway scene in the 1950s and 1960s, the last ones not being withdrawn until September 1967. The banging of the motion is a sound always associated with the Class, especially as they suffered from poor maintenance. Yet this was exactly the type of rough and ready working for which Riddles had designed them. Cleaner than usual, No 90457, allocated to Mirfield, heads a train of empty coal wagons back to Bold Colliery, and is seen leaving Liverpool past Edge Hill on Thursday 6 June 1963. This engine ended its work at Wakefield shed in January 1966. *JC*

Below This is not quite what it seems, for officially the 'Austerity' 2-8-0s were not supposed to work passenger trains. This is the nearest to it, for No 90423 is heading a lengthy empty stock train near Farington on the West Coast Main Line south of Preston in June 1962. It was a Widnes engine at the time, but finally ended its days allocated to Colwick, Nottingham, from where it was withdrawn on 26 December 1965. *PH*

Above More typical of the 'Austerity' 2-8-0s is No 90725 in the usual filthy condition. An extremely long train of empty wagons, possibly for the Rock Salt traffic from Winsford, is crossing the Manchester Ship Canal south of Warrington in May 1964. The locomotive was Bolton-allocated, and in July it moved on to Wigan Springs Branch. Then in January 1965 Aintree gained the 2-8-0, from where it was made redundant the following June. *PH*

Below A final look at the happenings at Birkenhead Woodside on Sunday 5 March 1967. Immaculate Standard '9F' 2-10-0 No 92234, still with its

Western Region colour-route availability sticker under the cab number, waits to leave on one of the specials to Chester. No 92234 had been built at Crewe and entered traffic in August 1958 allocated to the ex-GWR shed at Pontypool Road. It remained on the Western Region until 1963, and for three months in 1961 was stationed at Bromsgrove for Lickey Incline banking duties. In September 1963 it was at Tyseley, and this was the month the ex-GWR sheds in the Birmingham area became LMR property. After a spell at Banbury, No 92234 became a Saltley engine in October 1966, and two months later moved to Birkenhead. Here it was withdrawn in November 1967. *JC*

6. Liverpool Edge Hill Motive Power Depot

Edge Hill Motive Power Depot was situated in a maze of lines east of Edge Hill station, a 15-minute walk away. Access was gained through a long pedestrian tunnel at the end of Tiverton Street. The depot was the largest in Liverpool, with 20 roads at one end, in the 'old shed', and 12 at the 'new shed' end. The coaling stage and turntable were separated from the main shed area by a bridge carrying the lines out to the Waterloo area of Liverpool.

The building that survived into British Railways days dated from 1865 and had been erected by the LNWR. The main building was of brick and had the standard type of hipped roofs covering the 200-foot-long roads. Offices were provided at the rear as well as sheer-legs and a wheel-drop for heavy maintenance. Extensions to the original building were actioned in 1902 when a new brick structure was erected at the rear, extending a number of through roads. Known as the 'new' shed, it was in the later LNWR style with a glazed 'northlight'-pattern roof.

In 1914 a replacement coaling plant was built in ferro-concrete to a new unique design, and remained in use until the shed closed. It was served by a high-level line up which bottom-door-opening hopper wagons were pushed to replenish the bunker. This was divided into sections to hold different grades of coal, the best reserved for express engines. Smokeless fuel was also provided for locomotives working through the lengthy tunnels on trip workings from the docks to the Gridiron sidings. These sidings, close to the shed, had opened in 1882 and acquired the local 'Gridiron' name because of the shape of the layout. The new coaling plant enabled the time taken to refuel locomotives to be reduced to a few minutes and only needed the attention of nine men, each set working a 12-hour shift.

When the LMS was formed in 1923 a plan to modernise engine sheds under their command was formulated and Edge Hill received attention in 1934, when new ash plants were installed. In 1938 the 'old' shed received a new roof, and a water-softening plant was brought into use. The 'new' shed was re-roofed six years later and the shed remained in this condition until closure. British Railways chose not to spend money on any further improvements and the shed slowly decayed through the 1960s. Available money was spent in building a new depot for diesel and electric locomotives at Allerton.

Edge Hill was coded 8A by the LMS, and this remained unchanged throughout. The locomotives allocated to the shed reflected the workings it was responsible for, and covered the main passenger workings from the city, freight workings and parcels, as well as providing shunting engines to work the 'Gridiron' and other yards. When the Bowen Cooke '6F' 0-8-2Ts were built in 1911 a number of these became Edge Hill property, and they were joined by the Beames LMS-built '7F' 0-8-4Ts. There were still seven of these on allocation on the first day of British Railways ownership, the last example of this Class remaining at Edge Hill until withdrawal in December 1951.

The other notable 'last of class' operating from Edge Hill was 'Claughton' 4-6-0 No 46004, which went in April 1949, still bearing its LMS number 6004. This engine carried the official name *Princess Louise*, but this was removed in 1936 when 'Princess Royal' 4-6-2 No 6204 took the name. The 'Claughton' attracted the local nickname 'Waltzing Matilda', which was chalked upon it for a time. The last unrebuilt 'Royal Scot, 4-6-0, No 46137, was also an Edge Hill engine, and it was even entrusted to work the down 'Red Rose' on 30 June 1954. Although not allocated to Edge Hill, the unique turbine-driven 4-6-2 No 46202 was a regular visitor, Edge Hill being adopted as its second home.

One of the saddest losses was the wrecking of Edge Hill 'Jubilee' No 45637 *Windward Islands* in the Harrow disaster of Wednesday 8 October 1952 and the resulting tragic loss of life. The train involved was the 8.00 am Euston to Liverpool, known as the 'Liverpool Flyer', and was double-headed by No 45637 and 'Princess Royal' 4-6-2 No 46202; the latter had just been rebuilt from the turbine engine to conventional operation and named *Princess Anne*. Both engines were crewed by Edge Hill men. No 45637 had worked up from Liverpool the previous afternoon on a relief to the 2.10 pm to London, with Driver Albert Perkins and Fireman George Cowper. Camden decided to send the 'Jubilee' back home with the same crew on the 8.00 am piloting No 46202, which was a Camden engine crewed by Edge Hill's Driver Bill Darton and Fireman George Dowler. Driver Perkins lost his life in the horrific accident, but both firemen and Driver Darton miraculously survived. George Cowper had a particularly lucky escape as he was thrown through the air and landed on the 'Jubilee' framing; he carries the scars to this day, and was last heard of in Australia. George Dowler has only recently passed away.

To return to the locomotives at Edge Hill, details are given at the end of this book in the section on allocations at various dates, together with actual visit reports, giving a flavour of what could be seen. An interesting

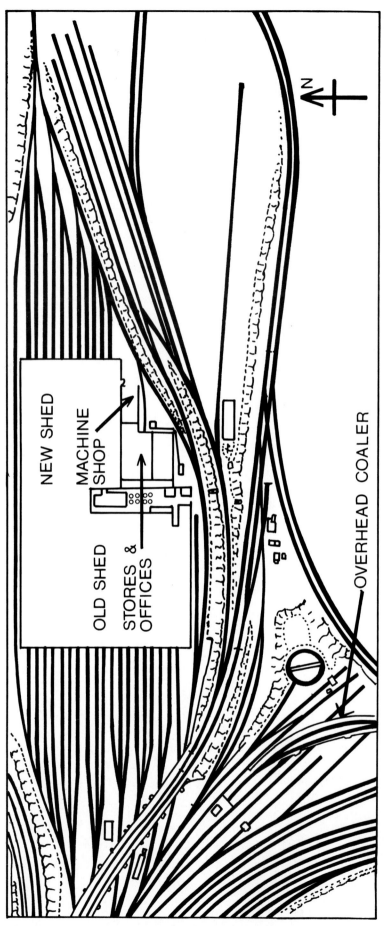

NEW SHED

MACHINE SHOP

OLD SHED

STORES & OFFICES

OVERHEAD COALER

N

Track plan of Liverpool Edge Hill motive power depot in 1950

point is that Edge Hill did not have British Railways Standard locomotives allocated, an unusual situation for a major steam depot. Standard locomotives did, however, work in, and Edge Hill would use them on their own turns of duty at various times.

The depot closed to steam from Monday 6 May 1968, bringing to an end an association with the steam locomotive that had lasted for over 100 years. The previous Friday, 3 May, had virtually seen the end of steam trips from the shed; the 9.00 pm Edge Hill (Wavertree Parcels Depot) to Blackburn, worked by Stanier 4-6-0 No 44777, and the 10.47 pm Edge Hill to Mold Junction freight, worked by Stanier 2-8-0 No 48374, were the last return workings off Edge Hill to other areas.

The last steam workings booked for 4 May were: 4.50 am Wavertree to Red Bank parcels, with 4-6-0 No 45187 to return light to Patricroft; 5.35 am Target 6, with 2-8-0 No 48293; 5.40 am Target 4, with 2-8-0 No 48715; 7.15 am Engineers, with 4-6-0 No 45305; 8.40 am empty coaching stock Kirkdale to Ardwick, with 4-6-0 No 45287, running light to Patricroft afterwards; and the 8.55 am Stanley to Bickershaw and Edge Hill freight, with 4-6-0 No 45156. On return to Edge Hill, No 45156 then shunted the locomotives on shed ready for their final departures.

On shed at 9.30 pm on 3 May were Stanier '5MT' 4-6-0s Nos 44777, 45055, 45156, 45187, 45231, 45284, 45287 and 45305, and Stanier '8F' 2-8-0s Nos 48045, 48056, 48168 (allocated to Heaton Mersey), 48293, 48294, 48374, 48467, 48529, 48665, 48692, 48722, 48746, 48752 and 48765, all on the active list. Withdrawn were Nos 44711, 44864, 44926, 45376, 48012, 48308, 48433 and 48614. No 48715 came on shed later after working the last Brunswick trip, while Nos 45284 and 48056 had their fires dropped for the last time on arrival. At the same time No 45055 was waiting by the coaler to leave light for Patricroft.

On Saturday 4 May at the same time, 9.30 pm, Nos 45187, 45287, 45305, 48293 and 48765 had gone. At 10.45 pm the very last diagrammed steam working from Edge Hill took place, with Stanier 4-6-0 No 44877, a Carnforth engine, leaving to work the 11.03 pm empty coaching stock from Downhill Sidings into Lime Street for the 12.10 am to Cardiff and 12.45 am to Glasgow. It then returned to Edge Hill after removing the empty stock

from the arrival from Penzance, which left Lime Street somewhat late due to a signal fault at 2.15 am on the Sunday.

The locomotives left at the shed were booked to leave for their new depots as follows: 4 May, No 48467 under its own steam; 5 May, 10.30 am, No 48168 hauling Nos 48529 and 45156; 10.45 am, No 44777 hauling Nos 48746 and 48665; and 4.00 pm, No 48374 hauling No 48692. At unspecified times during the day No 44877 hauled Nos 48715, 48752 and 45231 (a Carnforth engine), and Nos 48293 and 48294 left under their own steam. On shed on the Sunday in readiness for the Monday morning workings were the following diesels: Class '40' Nos D201, D223, D269, D301, D370, D385 and D389; Class '47' No D1845; Class '24' Nos D5061 and D5064; and Class '25' Nos D5155, D5291, D7569, D7575, D7639 and D7641. The shed continued in use as a signing-on point and diesel stabling point, and some of the steam locomotives remained in store for a few more months. On Sunday 23 June the following were still there, stored awaiting scrap: Nos 44711, 44864, 44926, 45284, 48045, 48056, 48308, 48614 and 48722.

So, the end for Edge Hill as a top-link steam shed had come, and with it went many of the characters that made up the workforce. People like No 1 passenger link drivers Jimmy Lee, Joss Williams, Snowy Roberts, and Billy Donaghue, who would step off his engine at Lime Street or Euston as spruce as though he was just starting his day's work. Then there was Jack Griffiths, one of the fitters, who was constantly happy and joking. Overseeing all was Bill Backhouse, the much respected Chief Maintenance Foreman, who retired when the shed closed. He always wore a trilby hat when inspecting the comings and goings on the shed, and passed away in 1988 after living alone with his memories.

Nowadays nothing remains of Edge Hill depot, the buildings having been demolished not long after closure.

A general view of Edge Hill depot in 1960, with, from the left, 'Royal Scot' 4-6-0 No 46134 *The Cheshire Regiment*, Stanier '5MT' 4-6-0 No 45197, and Fowler '4F' 0-6-0 No 43876, allocated to Bedford. With their backs towards us are a Standard '5MT' 4-6-0, an ex-LNWR 0-8-0, a 'Jinty' 0-6-0T and, over on the far right, facing forward, is a Stanier 2-6-0. *PH*

Above The 'coal hole' at Edge Hill is on the left of this view on Tuesday 9 March 1965, with a Standard '9F' 2-10-0 raising steam. 'Crab' 2-6-0 No 42859 from Birkenhead is carefully taking the 1 in 27 incline off the shed on one of the outlets to the main line. *JC*

Left Alongside the unique coaling plant is Fleetwood-allocated Stanier '8F' 2-8-0 No 48211, not long after a works visit by the look of it. The date is Friday 5 June 1964, and this is an early morning photograph, as it was only at this time of day that the sun was in the correct position for photography from this spot. Note that the lamp bracket is lower down than usual on the right-hand side of the smokebox door - this was to make it safer for enginemen, who would not have to climb so high on their engines under the wires. No 48211 lasted in service until the week-ended 18 November 1967, its last operating base being Rose Grove. *JC*

All the Steam Age clutter and dirt around the coaling stage is caught well in this photograph of 'Britannia' 4-6-2 No 70010, previously named *Owen Glendower*, in May 1966. Allocated to Kingmoor at the time, this was another of the Class that went new to the Great Eastern main line at Norwich in May 1951. It was withdrawn from Kingmoor during the week-ended 23 September 1967. *JC*

Left Hiding its face from the camera behind a cloud of steam at Edge Hill is the 'Britannia' with the longest name, No 70048 *The Territorial Army 1908-1958*. The date is Friday 5 April 1963 and No 70048 had just been transferred to Aston from Holyhead. This was another member of the Class to end its days at Carlisle Kingmoor, withdrawal coming during the week-ended 6 May 1967. *JC*

Below A distinguished and regular visitor to Edge Hill was Crewe North-allocated Standard 'Pacific' No 71000 *Duke of Gloucester*, caught on film at the shed on Tuesday 25 May 1961. The encroaching masts for the electrification can be seen in the background, marking the end for Edge Hill steam depot. *JC*

Right Edge Hill had its own allocation of 'Pacifics' of the Stanier variety, which were much liked by the enginemen. One of the Liverpool allocation, 'Princess Royal' Class No 46208 *Princess Helena Victoria*, is captured for posterity at Edge Hill in early August 1961. The engine had, along with No 46204 *Princess Louise*, been in store for a number of months before this photograph was taken, and both had their nameplates removed for safe keeping. Each had been examined on 4 July and returned to traffic a few days later with nameplates affixed. No 46204 did not remain in traffic for very long, as it was withdrawn during the week-ended 7 October 1961. No 46208 lasted longer, withdrawal taking place in October 1962. *JC*

Below Edge Hill was a regular host to visiting 'Princess Coronation' Class 'Pacifics' and this Tuesday 16 May 1961 scene shows Crewe North-allocated No 46235 *City of Birmingham* being prepared to work the 9.45 pm parcels to London. Edge Hill received four members of this Class on its own allocation at this time, No 46233 *Duchess of Sutherland* during September 1960, and Nos 46229 *Duchess of Hamilton*, 46241 *City of Edinburgh* and 46243 *City of Lancaster* in March 1961; they all remained at Edge Hill until withdrawal. September 1964 was the month that the last remaining members of the Class were withdrawn, including No 46235, which now resides in Birmingham Science Museum. A nice touch was the presentation of the nameplates from No 46247 *City of Liverpool* to Liverpool City Council, to be hung up in the Council Chamber. *JC*

Above A further study of a 'Duchess' at Edge Hill - this time it is No 46238 *City of Carlisle*, appropriately a Carlisle Upperby engine. The date is Thursday 13 September 1962. During the previous year, on Saturday 29 June, this engine caused an operating problem in the Liverpool area. It had been diagrammed to work a Glasgow to Liverpool Exchange express, timed to arrive at 7.19 pm. Leaving Ormskirk No 46238 slipped violently, and at Town Green & Aughton failed completely. WD 'Austerity' 2-8-0 No 90712, an Aintree engine, came to the rescue and pulled the whole train into the station. Records show that this was the first recorded visit of an engine of this Class to Exchange station since 1947, when No 46232 put in

an appearance. No 46238 was another withdrawal at the demise of the Class in September 1964. *JC*

Below Unrebuilt 'Patriot' 4-6-0 No 45550, allocated to Edge Hill, stands on shed at the 'new end' on Tuesday 23 May 1961. It moved on to Warrington Dallam two months later, then Lancaster in April 1962, and finally Carnforth the next month. Withdrawal came during the week-ended 1 December 1962, No 45550 having been the last of the unrebuilt examples to remain active. It was never named - the name *Sir Henry Fowler* had been selected for it, but for reasons not recorded it was not applied. *JC*

A day in July 1961 finds another unrebuilt un-named 'Patriot' 4-6-0 on shed, No 45510, wearing a 12B Carlisle Upperby shedplate. The 'old' shed roof can be seen in the background, still in good condition at this late hour in the shed's history. No 45510 had been built at Crewe in 1932 and originally numbered 6012. This was another locomotive withdrawn in 1962, going during the week-ended 9 June after it had moved to Lancaster depot. *JC*

Above A pleasing picture of Class '7P' rebuilt 'Patriot' 4-6-0 No 45512 *Bunsen* at rest on Edge Hill on Wednesday 4 November 1964. Note that the boss of the rear wheel of the front bogie is larger than the front one, which was a little piece of the original 'Patriot' before rebuilding. *JC*

Left Looking out: Edge Hill-based rebuilt 'Patriot' 4-6-0 No 45535 *Sir Herbert Walker KCB* in 1961. *JC*

Right Showing a clean face inside Edge Hill shed in April 1965 is Warrington Dallam-allocated Standard '9F' 2-10-0 No 92058. Note the shed roof detail, giving plenty of light into this, the newer part of the depot. No 92058 moved to Speke Junction in June 1967 and Carlisle Kingmoor two months later, its final home until withdrawn three months on. *JC*

Conflicting information on the front of Stanier '5MT' 4-6-0 No 44666 on shed on Saturday 20 August 1966. The painted shed code says 2A, which was then the code for Birmingham Tyseley, but the buffer beam says Saltley. It had been a Saltley engine until September 1965 when it trans- ferred to Tyseley. To add to the confusion, it had actually been transferred to Edge Hill during the week the photograph was taken, and there it remained until withdrawal in February 1967. *JC*

An interesting visitor to Edge Hill on Tuesday 9 March 1965 is Stanier '5MT' 2-6-0 No 42947, its tender stacked high with coal for a long trip ahead. Painted on the smokebox is the shedcode 9G, which then denoted Manchester Gorton. Built in November 1933, this engine had been allocated to Edge Hill from 12 February 1938 until 9 February 1940, when it went to Crewe South. Gorton shed closed in 1965 and No 42947 moved on to Heaton Mersey where it remained until withdrawal later the same year on 4 December. *JC*

Above A Stanier '8F' 2-8-0 by day. No 48280, Edge Hill-owned, on shed in May 1965. This example of the Class was withdrawn in May 1966. *JC*

Left A Stanier '8F' 2-8-0 by night. It is a very cold early morning on Wednesday 25 January 1967 and No 48681 has spent the night out of steam awaiting the dawn, but with little prospect of work that day. This was the engine's last year of existence, withdrawal coming during the week-ended 22 July from Northwich. *JC*

Above A visiting '8F' 2-8-0 from nearby Speke Junction shed, No 48722, in September 1965, seen here paired with a narrower smaller tender from a 'Jubilee' Class 4-6-0. This engine had originally been built to an LNER order in 1944 and was constructed at Brighton. The LNER gave it class type 06 with an initial number of 7668, later re-numbered 3117 in 1946 and again in 1947 to 3547. Transfer shortly after to LMS stock meant another re-numbering to 8722. Final re-numbering to 48722 occurred on 7 May 1949 and withdrawal came in May 1968, the engine being then on Edge Hill's allocation. *JC*

Right Inside Edge Hill shed in 1965 is Stanier '8F' 2-8-0 No 48200, not long after a Crewe Works visit in December 1964. It had been put through the works as part of a plan to place certain locomotives in a strategic reserve, and on return to Edge Hill was placed in store. This plan was abandoned, so No 48200 was returned to traffic. The star below the cabside number denoted that the wheels had been specially balanced for faster running on fitted freights. No 48200 ended at Bolton, withdrawal coming during the week-ended 13 January 1968. *JC*

The old order of freight movers is epitomised by the ex-LNWR '7F' 0-8-0. This example, No 49243, prepares to leave Edge Hill shed on Sunday 3 April 1960 for a special working in connection with engineering works. This old timer lasted until March 1961 at Edge Hill. *PH*

Above Another example of the LNWR 'G2' 0-8-0, No 49293, on Edge Hill shed on a pleasant evening in May 1962 looking rather work weary and unkempt. Although the boiler pressure was a modest 175 lbs, they were still powerful locomotives and did useful work plodding around Liverpool. No 49293 had its fire thrown out for the last time during the last week of November 1962. JC

Below Edge Hill had on its books for many years a couple of ex-Lancashire & Yorkshire Railway '2F' 0-6-0STs for working in Crown Street coal yard, where restricted clearances made this type of engine ideal. They were a rebuild by Aspinall of earlier Barton Wright tender engines. Here No 51441 basks in the winter sunshine on Friday 27 January 1961, recently transferred from Sutton Oak. It was withdrawn during the week-ended 18 March the same year. JC

The popular and hard-working LMS standard shunting engine, the 'Jinty' '3F' 0-6-0T. Here No 47357 awaits duty on Tuesday 14 September 1965. Withdrawal came during the week-ended 24 December 1966, when only five out of a Class total of 417 remained active. It remained stored at Edge Hill until May 1967, when it went for scrap at Barry Docks. However, it was rescued and now lives on in preservation at the Midland Railway Centre at Butterley. JC

A visitor from Doncaster shed, outside the 'new' shed at Edge Hill on Friday 4 June 1965, is clean 'B1' Class 4-6-0 No 61326. It had been on shed for the week for repairs to the firebox stays. This engine had been built by the North British Locomotive Company after nationalisation and entered traffic at Gorton on 8 June 1948. An interesting move during the week-ended 12 August 1950 was across Manchester to the ex-LMS depot at Newton Heath, on loan until 30 September when it returned to Gorton. When it was withdrawn on 20 March 1966 it was still on allocation to Doncaster. *JC*

Left An unusual transfer to Edge Hill was this Fowler '2F' 0-6-0T No 47166, one of only ten introduced in 1928 with a short wheelbase for dock shunting. It had been transferred from Bidston just before this photograph was taken in May 1961, and awaits fitting of an 8A shedplate. It proved to be a very useful engine as shed pilot, shunting dead engines around the yard and wash-out roads. It was withdrawn during the week-ended 11 May 1963, and was then stored at Edge Hill until October when it went to Horwich Works for scrapping. *JC*

Below The graceful lines of a Stanier masterpiece are beautifully caught in this view of ex-works 'Jubilee' 4-6-0 No 45629 *Straits Settlements*, belonging to Crewe North shed, at Edge Hill on Sunday 31 May 1959. Dating back to November 1934, it had first operated from Manchester Longsight. In the early 1950s it was at Trafford Park, and returned to Longsight by 1957. In June 1958 it went to Crewe North, where it stayed until May 1962 when Carnforth received the engine. Carlisle Kingmoor was its last operating base, going there in June 1963 until withdrawal during the last week in April 1965 after a period in store. It was towed north to the Motherwell Machinery & Scrap Co at Wishaw for scrap the following August. *PH*

Our final look at Edge Hill shows Stanier '5MT' 4-6-0 No 45156 *Ayrshire Yeomanry* about to back off the shed on the Saturday morning of 20 April 1968 to work the RCTS 'The Lancastrian No 2' railtour. Local members of the Merseyside branch of the RCTS had been allowed to clean and paint the locomotive specially for this moment during the preceding weeks, and the excellent results can be seen here. The nameplates and front number-plate were wooden replicas made by one of the RCTS team.

The tour of 279 miles started from Lime Street at 8.54 am and took the original Liverpool & Manchester route through Huyton Junction to Wigan North Western. The ten-coach special then set off to Preston and took the Fylde line through Poulton to Fleetwood. Here 'Britannia' No 70013 took over to work its way back to Preston, using various junctions so as to be facing north. The tour then ran through to Oxenholme for a run down the branch to Windermere, where No 70013 was watered and turned. The next destination was Morecambe Promenade station, where No 45156 was waiting to take the train to Heysham Harbour. After return to Morecambe, and the turning of *Ayrshire Yeomanry*, another 'Black Five', No 45342, joined the tour and with No 45156 double-headed back to Carnforth and through Wennington, Settle Junction and Hellifield. Then through Blackburn and back again to Preston, where No 70013 was waiting to take over for the run to Liverpool Exchange station via Southport. The train arrived back only 30 minutes late after 11$\frac{1}{2}$ hours on the road, and with a happy but begrimed Inspector Donald Norman of Edge Hill who had accompanied the footplate crews throughout.

No 45156 remained at Edge Hill until the shed closed to steam the following month, moving on to Patricroft. On the closure of Patricroft on 1 July 1968, the final move was to Rose Grove until withdrawal on the last day of steam operation in August. JC

7. Shed portraits: Scottish Region

Above The Glasgow & South Western Railway's engine shed at Ayr was built in a distinctive stone design as can be seen in this photograph dated July 1964. The LMS coded Ayr 30D and this was changed to 67C from 1 January 1949. On parade outside the shed are three of the allocation of 'Crab' 2-6-0s, Nos 42916 (withdrawn 19 June 1965), 42913 (withdrawn 26 June 1966) and 42909 (withdrawn 17 January 1966). Hiding in the shed is 42919, withdrawn on 3 October 1966. The depot's association with this class was a long one, with seven being on allocation on 1 January 1948. This had grown to 17 by May 1965, by then the largest allocation of this type anywhere. A visit to the shed on Saturday 27 August 1966 found that there were still five on the active list, Nos 42737, 42789, 42795, 42803 and 42919 all working on the day. Steam operation ceased at Ayr on Monday 3 October 1966, 25 diesels based at Ayr taking over from 45 steam locomotives at Ayr and nearby Hurlford. JC

Left Glasgow Polmadie shed in July 1965, with Standard '4MT' 2-6-0 No 76070 on shed. This engine spent all its life at Scottish sheds, being delivered to Motherwell from Doncaster Works in September 1956. It had a period on banking duties at Beattock from April until December 1964, when it finally settled at Polmadie. It was withdrawn on 17 August 1966. JC

One of the interesting features of the last years of steam operation was the allocation of unusual locomotives to sheds not usually associated with the type. One such occurrence was the transfer to the ex-Caledonian Railway Polmadie shed in September 1963 of six ex-LNER-design 'A2' Class 'Pacifics', Nos 60512, 60522, 60524, 60527, 60530 and 60535. They had come from Edinburgh and were used on turns that had previously been worked by the 'Duchess' 'Pacifics'.

This view, taken 'over the wall' in Polmadie Road just before the entrance to the shed, shows No 60535, formerly named *Hornets Beauty*, at the back of the shed in July 1965, having been withdrawn the previous month. All the Polmadie 'A2s' had gone by the end of June, all withdrawn except No 60530, which had been transferred to Dundee in August 1964. Polmadie closed to steam on 1 May 1967. JC

Above Dunfermline shed, coded 62C under British Railways, was situated on the south side of the line east of Dunfermline Upper station and was of North British Railway origin. New coaling and ash plants were put into use in February 1952, and the following photographs show these facilities being put to use by Dunfermline engines, all on 6 July 1965. 'B1' Class 4-6-0 No 61101 waits alongside with Gresley-designed 'J38' 0-6-0 No 65934 under the coaler. Both engines were withdrawn on 31 December 1966. *JC*

Left Another look at No 65934, now conveniently moved forward for a better view. *JC*

On the ashpits at Dunfermline is WD 'Austerity' 2-8-0 No 90229, with the trolleys for removing the waste alongside. This was an area at many depots that could become a real eyesore, with mounds of smouldering fire remains everywhere. With the modern equipment, Dunfermline looks very neat and tidy. No 90229 was withdrawn on 2 September 1966 and was scrapped at McWilliams yard, Shettleston, three months later. JC

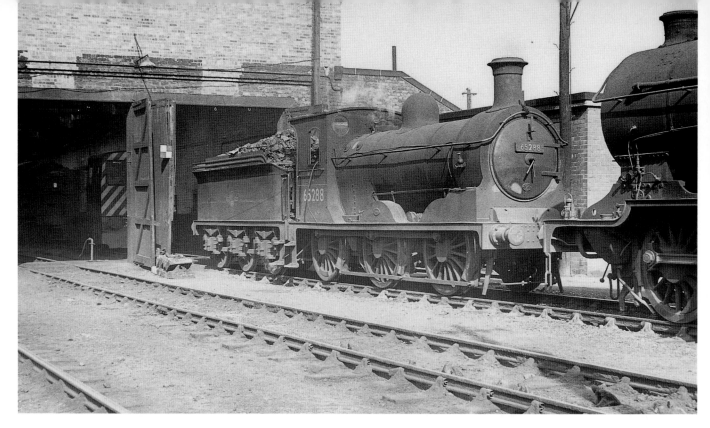

Above Dunfermline shed was re-roofed in the 1950s, and evidence of the newer brickwork can be seen in this view of 'J36' Class 0-6-0 No 65288 standing outside, again on Tuesday 6 July 1965. This engine was a remarkable survivor considering that its design dated back to 1888. Along with 'J36' No 65345 at nearby Thornton Junction, it lasted to the very final day of normal steam operation in Scotland, 1 May 1967. This was the day that Dunfermline officially closed to steam, but Nos 65288 and 65345 were not actually withdrawn until 5 June, therefore being the last two steam locomotives in Scottish stock. *JC*

Below We now move to Edinburgh for a visit to Dalry Road shed, the ex-Caledonian Railway depot serving Princes Street station. This view shows the proximity of Dalry Road station, which afforded an excellent view of locomotives at the wooden coaling stage. 'B1' Class 4-6-0s were allocated to the depot, including this one, No 61007 *Klipspringer*, heading a line of locomotives being replenished in this August 1961 view. No 61007 moved on to St Margarets the next month, and Glasgow Eastfield in December 1962, from where it was withdrawn on 6 February 1964. *JC*

Another 'B1' on shed at Dalry Road, this time No 61307, in July 1965. When the shed closed on 4 October of that year the remaining 13 engines, including No 61307, transferred to St Margarets. No 61307 was finally withdrawn on 19 November 1966. JC

Above Perth shed in August 1962, with the coaling tower dominating this view of Edinburgh Haymarket-based 'A1' Class 4-6-2 No 60162 *Saint Johnstoun*. Perth had an allocation of around 80 locomotives at this time, and visitors from many of the Scottish sheds always added to the interest. This engine remained at Haymarket from 23 December 1949, when it had arrived new from Doncaster Works, through to 8 September 1963, when Haymarket closed to steam. It then transferred to St Margarets, but could not find useful employment, so was withdrawn seven weeks later on 28 October. *JC*

Below A reminder of Perth shed's origins as part of the Caledonian Railway is seen in the shape of ex-Caledonian Pickersgill '3P' 4-4-0 No 54466 in August 1962. This was something of a rare find at this late date, as only one other, No 54463, remained, at Glasgow Polmadie. No 54466 had spent many years allocated to Aviemore, being withdrawn from there on 12 March 1962. It had arrived at Perth for storage just before this photograph was secured and remained there until October 1963, when it made its last journey to Arnott Young's yard at Troon for breaking up. *JC*

Above Carstairs shed in August 1962, with Carlisle Kingmoor 'Royal Scot' 4-6-0 No 46128 *The Lovat Scouts* waiting for work at the north end of the shed. This was another ex-Caledonian Railway shed that had been rebuilt by the LMS in 1934. The LMS code was 28E, and this was changed to 64D under British Railways. Another change in 1960 to 66E brought Carstairs under the control of Polmadie instead of Edinburgh St Margarets. The shed closed on 31 December 1966 and the final allocation was as follows: Fairburn '4MT' 2-6-4T Nos 42125 and 42694; Stanier '5MT' 4-6-0 Nos 44953, 45084, 45161, 45365 and 45478; 'B1' 4-6-0 No 61008; Standard '5MT' 4-6-0 No 73108; and Standard '4MT' 2-6-0 No 76113. All were withdrawn on the day. *JC*

Below Carlisle Canal shed on Monday 7 August 1961. Standing inside is the last active 'D34' 'Glen' Class 4-4-0, No 62484 *Glen Lyon*, down from Hawick shed. It was withdrawn on 6 November 1961 and was stored at Hawick until April 1962, then moved to Bathgate for further storage. In April 1963 it moved to Arnott Young's yard at Old Kilpatrick for scrapping. Canal shed was of North British Railway origin and changed shed codes and regions during its British Railways ownership. Starting as part of the Scottish Region and coded 'CAR', from 1 January 1950 it moved to the LMR and became 12B; not for long though, for on 1 July 1951 it returned to the Scottish Region as 68E. From 23 February 1958 it returned to the LMR's control as 12D, then 12C from 20 April the same year until closure on 17 June 1963. *PH*

8. Shed portraits: London Midland Region

The most northerly of LMR depots was Carlisle Kingmoor. The brick building we see here was brought into use in 1917, replacing an earlier Caledonian Railway wooden structure on the same site. This was another shed that changed regions under British Railways. On nationalisation it was coded 12A, then on 1 January 1949 it became Scottish Region property under code 68A. It returned to its old code 12A and back into LMR territory on 23 February 1958 until closure on 1 January 1968. During its last year of operation it attracted many visits from enthusiasts to see over 100 steam engines 'on shed' on a Sunday afternoon. Today nothing remains of the shed, the site now having become a nature reserve.

Our first view of the south end of the shed is on Thursday 30 May 1963 with Kingmoor-based 'Princess Coronation' 'Pacific' No 46255 *City of Hereford* on main-line standby duty. Alongside is Ivatt '4MT' 2-6-0 No 43103. No 46255 remained at Kingmoor until withdrawal in September 1964. *JC*

At virtually the same spot on Sunday 29 July 1962 is a visitor from Polmadie, but renewing acquaintance with its old home, Stanier 4-6-0 No 44719. This locomotive had been built at Crewe and entered traffic at Edge Hill on 19 March 1949, moving on to Kingmoor three weeks later on 9 April. Here it remained until October 1952 when the engine transferred to Inverness. It obviously liked the Highland scenery, for it did not get transferred again until April 1961, when Polmadie claimed it. The final move was to Grangemouth in July 1964 from where No 44719 was withdrawn on 30 October the same year. Note the fire bucket hanging on the water column for use in winter to stop the water from freezing. *JC*

Right Alongside No 44719 on the same date is 'Royal Scot' 4-6-0 No 46145 *The Duke of Wellington's Regt (West Riding)*, which had been allocated to Leeds Holbeck the week before. This engine had originally been named *Condor*, and had been built by the North British Locomotive Company in 1927; the name was changed to the one carried here in 1935. The conversion to double chimney and 2A-type boiler came about in 1944. The year 1962 was not a good one for the 'Scots', as 29 members of the 71-strong Class were withdrawn, including No 46145, which ceased operation on 3 December. *JC*

Below A reminder that Scotland was not far away was the allocation of Standard 'Clan' 'Pacifics' to Kingmoor. Another 29 July 1962 photograph finds No 72008 *Clan MacLeod* in light steam taking a Sunday rest.

Allocated new to the depot from Crewe Works in February 1952, it remained at Carlisle until withdrawal on 16 April 1966. *JC*

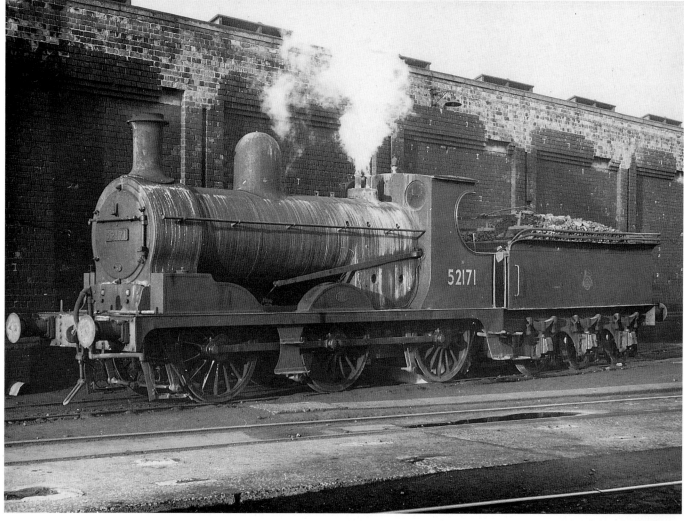

Left A final view at Kingmoor on 29 July 1962, with LMS '4F' 0-6-0 No 44305 on show at the north end of the shed. A Crewe Works production of 1926, No 44305 remained at Kingmoor from when this photograph was taken until withdrawal during the week-ended 3 April 1965, having been in store since the previous November. *JC*

Below left Aintree shed on Sunday 21 February 1960, with ex-Lancashire & Yorkshire Railway Aspinall-designed '3F' 0-6-0 No

52171 on show, looking very much in need of a tidy-up. This 1889 vintage engine had transferred to Aintree from Lostock Hall in March 1951, and remained in service at the shed until the week-ended 20 May 1961. Aintree shed opened in 1886 and was re-roofed in 1937, the difference in brick still being apparent in the shed wall in this view. It was coded 23B from 1935 until 1 January 1950, when it changed to 27B, and then one final change in September 1963 to 8L. Closure came on 12 June 1967. *PH*

Above Walton-on-the-Hill was a Cheshire Lines Committee shed situated on the freight line from Fazakerley Junction to Huskisson Goods Yard. There had once been a station at Walton, but this had closed in 1918. If you used the train, visits to the shed had to be made from Walton Junction LMS station, followed by a 10-minute walk to Queens Drive, where the entrance could be found. Under British Railways managership it was coded 'WAL' on 1 January 1948, changing to 13F from 1 January 1950, and to 27E from 22 May the same year. A change to 8R was made from 9 September 1963, but this did not last long, as the shed closed three months later on 15 December.

The allocation was around 20 locomotives and included members of the 'J10' Class, a Parker design for the Manchester, Sheffield & Lincolnshire Railway dating from 1892. This example, No 65133, was photographed at Walton on Sunday 19 April 1959 standing in the part of the shed from which the roof had been removed in 1952, reducing the shed from six to four roads. No 65133 had transferred to Walton from Gorton in February 1948 and remained on allocation until withdrawal. Although looking derelict in this view, it was still officially on the active list, for withdrawal was officially given eight months later as 12 December. *PH*

Left Next we move to Crewe North on Sunday 27 March 1960 to see 'Princess Coronation' 4-6-2 No 46222 *Queen Mary* belonging to Polmadie on the 70-foot turntable. In the background is the modern semi-roundhouse, which was constructed as part of the 1953 modernisation plan. Closure came on 24 May 1965, and the final allocation of 38 locomotives were all transferred away as follows: to Crewe South, Stanier '5MT' 4-6-0 Nos 44678, 44679, 44680, 44681, 44683, 44685, 44765 and 45243, and 'Britannia' 4-6-2 Nos 70000, 70010, 70012, 70014, 70017, 70018, 70019, 70020, 70021, 70023, 70024, 70025, 70027, 70028, 70030, 70031, 70033, 70034, 70042, 70043, 70044, 70046, 70050, 70051, 70052 and 70054; to Stoke, Ivatt '2MT' 2-6-2T Nos 41212 and 41229; and to Stockport Edgeley, 'Britannia' 4-6-2 Nos 70004 and 70015. *PH*

Below Crewe South shed on the same day sees Nuneaton-based ex-LNWR 'G2' 0-8-0 No 49440, with a tender cab, keeping company with 'Crab' 2-6-0 No 42843. The allocation at this time was over 100 locomotives, and much more varied than could be found at the North shed, as South was mainly involved in freight and parcels working. It was also the collection point for engines entering Crewe Works. A standard LNWR straight shed, open at both ends and with 12 roads, it was opened in 1897. The shed roof was replaced under British Railways and the covered accommodation reduced to eight roads. Coded 5B from 1935, final closure came on 6 November 1967. No 49440 shuffled around the Nuneaton area until being withdrawn during the week-ended 24 March 1962. No 42843 managed to work until 30 March 1963, its last base being Fleetwood. *PH*

Above Crewe South on Sunday 26 June 1960, with 'Patriot' 4-6-0 No 45518 *Bradshaw* on shed. It carries the new code for Aston shed, 21D, which had been changed from 3D the week before. No doubt John Corkill was familiar with this locomotive, for in 1959 it was part of the Edge Hill allocation, moving on to Warrington in February 1960. Aston received No 45518 at the beginning of June and sent it back to Edge Hill in September 1961. It moved to its final allocation, Lancaster, in February 1962 and was withdrawn the same year on 20 October. *JC*

Right Part of the Crewe district was Stoke-on-Trent shed, coded 5D from 1935 until closure on 7 August 1967. Its origins went back to North Staffordshire Railway days, and the six-road straight shed was brought into use in 1870. There was already a roundhouse in use on the opposite side of the line that ran past the shed to Stoke station. Around 100 locomotives were allocated in the 1950s, and this included a large contingent of '4F' 0-6-0s of Midland and LMS origin. At nationalisation there were 29 on strength, and in March 1959 no fewer then 32. This view at Stoke shed on 26 June 1960 shows a line of these locomotives headed by Burton-based Fowler 0-6-0 No 43991. This engine finished its days at Westhouses shed in May 1965, where it was stored until September and cut up the next month at Draper's yard, Hull. *JC*

Left The other extreme in the Crewe district was the little shed at Uttoxeter, another former North Staffordshire Railway establishment that had opened in 1901. It had the code 5F from 1935 until closure on 7 December 1964, and maintained an allocation of around seven engines, mainly used on local passenger workings. This view of the shed was recorded on Sunday 26 June 1960, and includes Stanier 2-6-4T No 42593, visiting from Stoke, and from Crewe South LMS '4F' 0-6-0 No 44592. The allocation on the day that this photograph was taken was '4MT' 2-6-4T Nos 42358, 42375, 42605 and 42665, and '4F' 0-6-0 Nos 44355 and 44357. *JC*

Below far left Wellingborough shed on Sunday 15 May 1960, showing the Midland Railway style of architecture. This is Wellingborough No 1 roundhouse, which opened in 1868. Another roundhouse, No 2 shed, was opened in 1872 on the same site, but was a separate building. No 1 shed was demolished in 1964, but No 2 still stands today. Coded 15A from 1935, it became 15B in September 1963 and finally closed to steam on 13 June 1966. Here we have Standard '9F' 2-10-0 No 92105, which came to the shed new from Crewe Works on 8 September 1956. It moved to Kettering two months later where it remained until March 1963, then returning to Wellingborough. Kettering again became its home in January 1964, then 92105 moved to Leicester Midland nine months later. In May 1965 it moved to Birkenhead, where it remained until withdrawal in January 1967. *PH*

Above Graphically illustrating the poor working conditions associated with the last years of steam working is this 1957 view at Hasland shed, coded 18C. On the turntable is Ivatt '2MT' 2-6-0 No 46499, which was a Hasland-allocated engine. Also in view is 1932-introduced Kitson-built 0-4-0ST No 47003, which ended its duties on the Western Region at Swansea East Dock. Hasland was the Midland Railway's Chesterfield depot and was a standard roundhouse design, opened in 1875. Because of subsidence caused by the local coal-mining industry, the roof became unstable and had to be removed in the 1950s, leaving the interior open to the elements as can be seen here. Hasland had an allocation of the mighty Beyer-

Garratt locomotives, and had the distinction of operating the last one, No 47994, which left for scrapping at Crewe Works on 14 March 1958.

At nationalisation it had an allocation of 54 locomotives, but this had dropped to 39 by April 1959. It was re-coded 16H on 9 September 1963 and final closure came on 7 September 1964. The final allocation and distribution on closure day was as follows: withdrawn, LMS '4F' 0-6-0 Nos 44381, 44463 and 44603; to Westhouses, '4F' 0-6-0 Nos 43967, 43982, 44054 and 44235, and LMS '3F' 0-6-0T Nos 47535, 47543 and 47611; too Wigan Springs Branch, Stanier '8F' 2-8-0 No 48187; and to Bolton, Stanier '8F' 2-8-0 No 48205. The one diesel shunter, D3792, went to Toton. *JC*

9. Shed portraits: Eastern Region

Above Our first visit to an Eastern Region depot is to Doncaster, which was a 12-road through shed opened by the Great Northern Railway in 1876. On 5 April 1959 we see Doncaster-based 'A1' 4-6-2 No 60158 *Aberdonian* - note the damaged cylinder casing. This was a November 1949 production from Doncaster Works, going initially to King's Cross. It remained in service until 26 December 1964 still at Doncaster. *PH*

Below The old order at Doncaster. On shed on Sunday 28 February 1960 is '04/1' Class '7F' 2-8-0 No 63617 in the usual filthy state for this Class. This was a visitor from Frodingham, where it remained on allocation until withdrawal on 12 December 1962. This was one of the Robinson Great Central type introduced in 1911 with Belpaire boiler. *PH*

Doncaster shed was re-roofed in the 1950s in the style we see here, and coded 36A by British Railways. It was the last depot to operate steam locomotives on the Eastern Region. On nationalisation day it had an allocation of 190 locomotives, but when the shed closed to steam on 17 April 1966 the allocation was down to 32. All were withdrawn on that day, and the final allocation was as follows: 'B1' 4-6-0 Nos 61042, 61121, 61158, 61250, 61329, 61360 and 61406; 'O4' 2-8-0 Nos 63653, 63781, 63818 and 63858; WD 'Austerity' 2-8-0 Nos 90001, 90002, 90013, 90018, 90037, 90063, 90075, 90154, 90156, 90369, 90410, 90437, 90471, 90538, 90551, 90636, 90675 and 90709; and Standard 2-10-0 Nos 92146, 92172 and 92182. This photograph is dated Sunday 5 April 1959, and shows the unique 'W1' 4-6-4 No 60700, which had been rebuilt in 1937 from Gresley's experimental 'Hush Hush' four-cylinder compound with water-tube boiler. It remained at Doncaster until withdrawal two months later on 1 June. *PH*

Above Alongside one of the two old coaling stages at Doncaster, put out of use when the LNER erected a new concrete plant in the 1930s, is 'J50' Class '4F' 0-6-0T No 68963. The date is 28 February 1960. No 68963 transferred to the North Eastern Region shed at Ardsley on 3 August 1961, then on to Bradford Low Moor in December. From here it was withdrawn on 13 February 1962. *JC*

Below Down from Immingham shed and in very good condition, apart from a missing cylinder cover, is 'B1' 4-6-0 No 61379 *Mayflower*. The date is Sunday 5 March 1961. *Mayflower* was a regular visitor to Doncaster shed and remained on allocation at Immingham until withdrawal on 6 August 1962. *JC*

Above Our last look at Doncaster, again on 5 March 1961, shows 'A4' Class 4-6-2 No 60030 *Golden Fleece*, King's Cross-allocated, keeping company with 'A1' Class 4-6-2 No 60124 *Kenilworth*, ex-works awaiting return to Heaton shed. *JC*

Below Peterborough New England shed on 15 May 1960, and a clean WD 'Austerity' 2-8-0 is certainly worth a photograph. No 90133, allocated to Frodingham, looks powerful at the north end of the shed in the morning sun. This engine had been at Frodingham since transfer from Immingham on 26 May 1951, and remained there until withdrawn on 17 October 1965. It remained in store until March 1966 when it went to Arnott Young's yard at Dinsdale for scrap. New England closed to steam in January 1965. *PH*

Left Manchester Gorton shed, the heart of the Great Central Railway. Opened in 1879, it was the largest depot on the GCR with 20 undercover stabling roads. When British Railways took it over on 1 January 1948 it had an allocation of 159 locomotives, 40 of which were ex-GCR 'O1' Class 2-8-0s. Coded 39A from 1 January 1950, it remained virtually unchanged until the LMR took control from 1 February 1958, when 99 locomotives were on allocation. It was initially re-coded 9H, but this was changed shortly afterwards to 9G, which code it retained up to closure on 14 June 1965.

The final allocation of 43 locomotives were all transferred to other sheds as follows: to Newton Heath, 'Crab' 2-6-0 Nos 42700, 42715, 42831, 42905 and 42938, and Stanier '8F' 2-8-0 Nos 48543 and 48557; to Trafford Park, Fowler '4MT' 2-6-4T Nos 42327 and 42334, Stanier '8F' 2-8-0 No 48178, and Standard '2MT' 2-6-0 Nos 78007, 78011, 78012, 78014, 78023 and 78062; to Heaton Mersey, Stanier '5MT' 2-6-0 Nos 42945, 42947, 42950, 42951, 42955, 42958, 42960, 42961, 42964, 42967, 42968, 42974, 42975, 42977, 42978, 42980, 42981 and 42982;

and Stanier '8F' 2-8-0 Nos 48176, 48322, 48355, 48401, 48490, 48515, 48701 and 48748; and to Lower Darwen, 'Crab' 2-6-0 No 42878.

This view at Gorton was obtained on Saturday 8 April 1961 and shows '04/1' 2-8-0 No 63573 surrounded by LMS engines at its home shed. It only lasted a few weeks longer, for withdrawal came on 29 April. *PH*

Below left A look at March depot on Sunday 15 May 1960. There had been a depot at this Cambridgeshire location since 1884, and steam was finally banished in 1963. Coded 31B under British Railways, it maintained a sizeable allocation, 193 locomotives being on its books on 1 January 1948. Here we see a type associated with East Anglia for many years, the 'B17' Class 4-6-0. They lasted until 1960, and here we see No 61660, a 'B17/4' 'Footballer', which had been named *Hull City*, but has had the nameplates removed for safe keeping. This was the last of its Class in service and probably did not work again, even though its tender is full, for it had only three more weeks on the active list, official withdrawal coming on 2 June. *PH*

Above On the same day the sleek lines of Gresley 'O2/2' 2-8-0 No 63943 cannot be disguised under the grime. It had come down from Doncaster and is posed alongside the March landmark, the coaling tower. In 1948 March had 16 of this Class on allocation, but all were transferred away to Doncaster and Grantham in May and June 1950, replaced by WD 'Austerity' 2-8-0s. No 63943 was withdrawn on 22 September 1963. *PH*

10. Shed portraits: Southern Region

Exmouth Junction was the ex-LSWR establishment, a bus ride away from Exeter. A large allocation of over 100 locomotives was maintained through to the 1960s, when its importance rapidly diminished. Coded 72A, in December 1962 it became part of the Western Region and coded 83D. Closure came in May 1965, when the allocation of 23 locomotives was dispersed. During its heyday Bulleid 'Pacifics' formed a large part of the allocation, with 39 on strength at nationalisation. This photograph, taken on Thursday 30 July 1959, shows unrebuilt 'West Country' 4-6-2 No 34030 *Watersmeet* on shed. The engine was one of 40 'Pacifics' still allocated at the time. No 34030 was built in May 1946 and first operated from Ramsgate shed. It then transferred to Exmouth Junction in 1947 and remained there until withdrawal in September 1964. *PH*

From one of the largest depots on the Southern to one of the smallest, Wadebridge in Cornwall. It maintained around five locomotives, three of which were the much photographed 1874 vintage Beattie 2-4-0 'well tanks'. Inside the shed on Monday 27 July 1959 is No 30585, buffered up to 'O2' 0-4-4T No 30236, the other type allocated. Exmouth Junction's 'N' Class 2-6-0 No 31842 looks in. No 30585 was secured for preservation and can now be seen at Quainton Road, Buckinghamshire. Wadebridge changed to Western Region control at the same time as Exmouth Junction, and closed in November 1964. The buildings were demolished in 1969. *PH*

Bournemouth shed on 5 September 1966, with only two steam locomotives on view, Standard '4MT' 2-6-4T No 80085 and a Bulleid 'Pacific' in the background. The buildings we see here dated from 1935 when the Southern rebuilt the old LSWR shed dating from 1885. The roof was renewed by British Railways in the 1950s. At nationalisation the allocation was 58 locomotives, but this was down to 39 in 1965. The shed closed at the end of Southern steam in July 1967 and the site is now a car park. JC

Left Eastleigh depot is the location for the next two illustrations. The first shows lined-out 'USA' 0-6-0T No 30073 on shed on Wednesday 7 September 1966. This was a class of 14 locomotives acquired from the War Department in 1947 and used at Southampton Docks. They had been built in 1942 and 1945 in the USA by two companies, Porters and Vulcans. When the dock shunting was dieselised in 1963 a number of the Class were scrapped, but No 30073 survived on shed pilot duties at Eastleigh until withdrawal on 8 January 1967. Four of the Class remain in preservation. *JC*

Below Another modern tank engine design used on the Southern, the Ivatt '2MT' 2-6-2T. At Eastleigh is No 41294, which was built at Crewe Works in November 1951 and first allocated to Stewarts Lane. It spent its whole life on the Southern, ending at Eastleigh. This is another 7 September 1966 photograph, and although the locomotive looks in fine form, this may have been its last steaming, for it was withdrawn three days later. *JC*

11. Shed portraits: Western Region

Bath Green Park depot on Saturday 21 March 1959. By this time it was under Western Region control, having transferred from Southern Region ownership on 23 February 1958 and being re-coded 82F from 71G. The locomotives allocated on that date reflect the S&D/LMS origins of the depot, comprising the following: LMS '2P' 4-4-0 Nos 40563, 40564, 40568, 40569, 40601, 40634, 40696, 40697, 40698 and 40700, Ivatt '2MT' 2-6-2T Nos 41241, 41242, 41243, 41248, 41249, 41296 and 41304, LMS '4F' 0-6-0 Nos 44096, 44102, 44146, 44417, 44422, 44523, 44557, 44558, 44559, 44560 and 44561, Stanier '5MT' 4-6-0 Nos 44917 and 45440 (the latter subsequently transferred to Edge Hill), Fowler S&D '7F' 2-8-0 Nos 53800 to 53810 inclusive, Johnson '1P' 0-4-4T No 58086, Standard '5MT' 4-6-0 Nos 73047, 73049, 73050, 73051 and 73052, and Standard '4MT' 4-6-0 Nos 75071, 75072 and 75073.

In this view we see Standard '3MT' 2-6-2T No 82041 drafted in by the Western Region that month from Bristol Bath Road; it remained at Bath until withdrawal in December 1965. Also on view, peering out of the stone-built shed erected by the Midland Railway, is Fowler 2-8-0 No 53806. Bath shed closed along with the S&D on 7 March 1966. The allocation on that day was all withdrawn and comprised: GWR '5700' 0-6-0PT Nos 3681 and 3758, LMS '3F' 0-6-0T Nos 47276 and 47506, and Stanier '8F' 2-8-0 Nos 48309, 48706 and 48760. *PH*

The first of the Fowler '7F' 2-8-0s for the S&D, built in 1914, was No 53800, seen here on Bath shed on 21 March 1959. It was also the first of the Class to be withdrawn in June 1959. *PH*

Left Exeter shed was not the usual place to find a 'King' Class 4-6-0, but on Thursday 30 July 1959 No 6015 *King Richard III* was there after failing on a down Paddington to Plymouth express. Exeter was a modest-sized GWR depot of four through roads and a repair shop. It opened in 1894 and maintained an allocation of around 30 locomotives. It closed in October 1963, but remained in use as a diesel stabling point. *PH*

Above Shrewsbury shed on Monday 18 May 1959, with Newton Abbot-based 'Castle' Class 4-6-0 No 5011 *Tintagel Castle* looking well-groomed after arrival on shed from the West Country. The run to Shrewsbury was the longest turn at Newton Abbot, requiring an engine in prime condition. Built in July 1927, No 5011 spent virtually all of its British Railways career at Newton Abbot, from 1 January 1948 until May 1960, when it moved to Reading. In November the same year it moved to Old Oak Common, from where it was withdrawn in September 1962. Shrewsbury depot closed to steam on 6 March 1967. *PH*

Right Another 'Castle' for GWR fans to enjoy, this time No 5072 *Hurricane*, photographed on Sunday 8 March 1959 at Wolverhampton Oxley shed. The turntable at Stafford Road shed had failed, so locomotives had to work up to Oxley for turning. No 5072 was new in June 1938 and first operated from Newton Abbot. Its final allocation was Stafford Road, whence it was withdrawn in October 1962. Oxley closed completely on 6 March 1967. *PH*

Left Wrexham Croes Newydd shed was situated in the triangle formed by the Ruabon-Wrexham-Brymbo lines, and opened in 1902. It was a standard 'northlight'-pattern roundhouse and was the last to be constructed in this form by the Great Western. It maintained an allocation of around 40 locomotives and moved over to LMR control in September 1963, finally closing on 5 June 1967, being the last depot to operate ex-GWR steam power. This view shows '7400' Class 0-6-0PT No 7428, still with 'GWR' on its tank, alongside the coaling stage on Sunday 30 August 1959. No 7428 was built in June 1937 and started life at Newport Ebbw Junction. It was transferred from Wrexham to Machynlleth in October 1960 and remained there until it was withdrawn exactly two years later. *PH*

Below left The second steam shed at Wrexham was at Rhosddu, situated on the west side of the line north of Wrexham Exchange station, where the GWR and LNER lines ran side by side. It was of Great Central Railway origin and was a six-road shed with an allocation of around 25 locomotives. At nationalisation it was part of the LNER and coded 'WRX'. Transfer to the LMR came on 1 January 1950, and it was re-coded 6E. Final transfer to the Western Region came on 23 February 1958, when the allocation was as follows: Stanier '3MT' 2-6-2T Nos 40073, 40085, 40086, 40106, 40110, 40126, 40128 and 40205, Ivatt '2MT' 2-6-2T Nos 41231, 41232, 41236,

41237 and 41244, Fowler '4F' 0-6-0 No 43877, LMS '4F' 0-6-0 Nos 44058 and 44307, LMS '3F' 0-6-0T Nos 47284 and 47491, 'J69' Class '2F' 0-6-0T No 68553, 'J72' Class '2F' 0-6-0T Nos 68671, 68714 and 68727, 'N5' Class '2MT' 0-6-2T Nos 69281, 69349 and 69362, and Standard '3MT' 2-6-2T Nos 82020 and 82021. It was then re-coded 84K until closure on 4 January 1960.

The allocation on the final day and its disposal was as follows, and reflects the Western influence: to Croes Newydd, '1600' 0-6-0PT No 1618, '2251' 0-6-0 No 3204, '5700' 0-6-0PT Nos 3749, 3760, 4683, 8734 and 9610, '5600' 0-6-2T Nos 5606, 5651 and 6610, and Stanier '3MT' 2-6-2T No 40126; to Machynlleth, Stanier '3MT' 2-6-2T Nos 40085, 40086, 40110 and 40205, and Standard '3MT' 2-6-2T Nos 82000 and 82031; to Wellington, Ivatt '2MT' 2-6-2T Nos 41231 and 41232; to Shrewsbury, Standard '3MT' 2-6-2T Nos 82020 and 82021; to Leamington Spa, Ivatt '2MT' 2-6-2T No 41285; to Stourbridge, '1600' 0-6-0PT No 1663; and to Southall, '1600' 0-6-0PT No 1669.

This view, taken on 30 August 1959, shows local resident '1600' Class 0-6-0PT No 1618 in part of the shed that had its roof removed by British Railways following fire damage. This modern tank engine had been constructed at Swindon after nationalisation in December 1949 and first went to Llanelly. It was withdrawn in May 1962 from Croes Newydd. *PH*

Above Another view at Wrexham Rhosddu on the same day, with another modern tank engine, Ivatt '2MT' 2-6-2T No 41285, being prepared for Monday morning work. This one was built in November 1950 at Crewe and spent its first month at Crewe North before moving on to Sutton Oak. Withdrawal came in December 1966 from Carlisle Upperby. *PH*

12. Locomotive works portraits

Above Standing outside the Crewe Works paint shop on Sunday 12 April 1959 is 'Royal Scot' 4-6-0 No 46139 *The Welch Regiment*, after works attention and awaiting return to service at its home shed, Camden. Although in fine condition, it only remained in traffic until October 1962, its last shed allocation being Manchester Newton Heath. *PH*

Left Outside the Erecting Shop at Crewe on Sunday 30 October 1960 is another Camden-based 'Royal Scot', No 46146 *The Rifle Brigade*, soon to be re-united with its tender. This was another 1962 withdrawal, this time from Willesden in November. *JC*

Crewe Works in 1959, when over 100 steam locomotives would be on site. Inside the Erecting Shop is 'Princess Coronation' Class 4-6-2 No 46232 *Duchess of Montrose*, in for repair and painting into British Railways green livery. Just in front is 'Patriot' 4-6-0 No 45536 *Private W. Wood VC*. This would be the last visit for overhaul for Polmadie-based No 46232, as it was withdrawn in December 1962. *PH*

Fairburn '4MT' 2-6-4T No 42674 stands alongside one of the workshops at Crewe on Sunday 27 March 1960 after a light repair. This was the second one of the Class to be built at Derby Works in April 1945, and was first allocated to Walsall, moving to Stoke, then Birmingham Monument Lane, where it stayed until 1957. After a brief six months at Bushbury later in the year, it returned to Monument Lane and, in July 1959, went to Bangor. It moved back to Stoke in February 1960 where it remained until withdrawal during the week-ended 17 November 1962. It returned to its birthplace for scrapping. *PH*

Above Crewe Works had a motley collection of works shunters, usually older locomotives retired from other parts of the system. This example, No 52218, is an ex-Lancashire & Yorkshire Aspinall '3F' 0-6-0, a design that looked distinctly old-fashioned by the time this photograph was taken on 6 November 1961. It was one of the last of the Class to survive and shunted around the Crewe Works complex from its transfer in from Aintree in July 1953 until withdrawal in May 1962. *JC*

Right Ex-LNWR 'G2' 0-8-0 No 49262 awaits a decision on its future at Crewe on Thursday 12 April 1962. It had been withdrawn, although not officially until 8 December 1962, from its last shed, Buxton. In front is No 49404 from Edge Hill, seen in action earlier on page 43, and this was condemned during the next fortnight. *JC*

Above Horwich Works, not far from Bolton, also had elderly shunters, and this example is an ex-Lancashire & Yorkshire Aspinall rebuilt 0-6-0 saddle tanks; what made them special was that they retained their LMS numbers. One of the five, No 11304, was photographed in October 1961, but only lasted in active service for a further two months. The very last one, No 11305, was not withdrawn until June 1964, and was then stored for a while at Bolton shed. *PH*

Below Outside the paint shop at Horwich in October 1961 waiting to return to Bury is Hughes/Fowler 'Crab' 2-6-0 No 42820. The high standard of the work carried out can be well seen here - yet for all that, the locomotive only lasted in service until the week-ended 18 April 1964. *PH*

Swindon Works, the cradle of the Great Western Railway. Standing in the weigh house on Sunday 22 March 1959 is ex-works 'County' Class 4-6-0 No 1019 *County of Merioneth*, Swindon-allocated, and 'King' Class 4-6-0 No 6005 *King George II*, allocated to Wolverhampton Stafford Road. The 'King' was withdrawn on 20 November 1962 and the 'County' in January 1963. *PH*

Left Bristol Bath Road 'Castle' Class 4-6-0 No 5062 *Earl of Shaftesbury* stands on one of the turntable roads at Swindon Works on 22 March 1959. Alongside is '6700' Class 0-6-0PT No 6730, which was already withdrawn. No 5062 only lasted until August 1962. *PH*

Below Doncaster Works on Sunday 5 March 1961, with 'A4' 4-6-2 No 60010 *Dominion of Canada* receiving attention. This engine was withdrawn on 29 May 1965 from Aberdeen Ferryhill, and was exported to Canada for preservation. Alongside is Standard '4MT' 2-6-0 No 76034, Norwich-allocated and new from Doncaster Works to Stratford in December 1953. This engine finished its career on the Southern at Guildford in September 1964. *JC*

Above Withdrawn on 3 March 1961, Gresley 'N2' class 0-6-2T No 69586, with condensing gear, awaits its fate at Doncaster on 5 March. Cutting up commenced on 19 March. *JC*

Below Complete, but awaiting cutting-up at Doncaster on Sunday 5 April 1959, is 'B17/4' 4-6-0 No 61648, with nameplates *Arsenal* removed but the distinctive 'half football' surviving on the splasher. The locomotive had been withdrawn from Stratford on 1 December 1958. *PH*

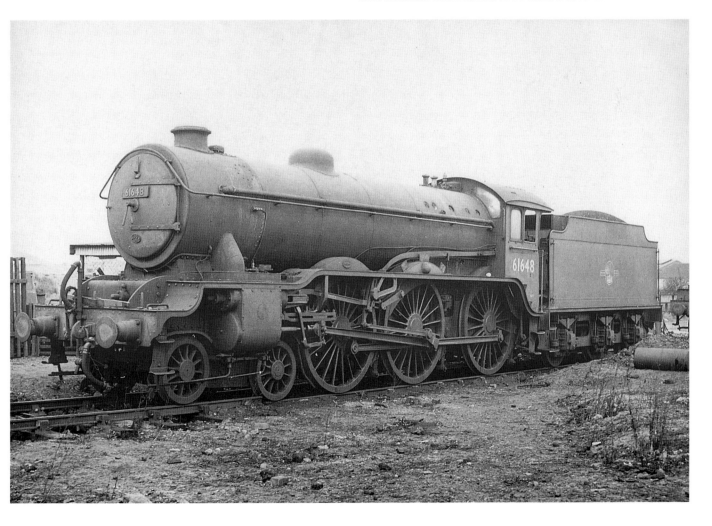

Stanier '5MT' 4-6-0 No 44999 beautifully out-shopped at Inverurie Works in July 1964, being fired up for its return to Perth. From 14 March to 29 August 1964 Inverurie had only out-shopped nine steam locomotives, Stanier 4-6-0 Nos 44880, 44999, 45011 and 45194, 'J37' 0-6-0 No 64620, 'J38' 0-6-0 No 65915, Standard '4MT' 2-6-0 Nos 76096 and 76114, and Standard '4MT' 2-6-4T No 80128, reflecting the decline in work on steam traction at this North of Scotland workshops. No 44999 was retained in service until 2 September 1966. JC

As a complete contrast, here are the remains of what was 'B17/6' 4-6-0 No 61649, once named *Sheffield United*, at Doncaster on 5 April 1959. Withdrawal from Ipswich had taken place on 10 February 1959. *PH*

13. Preserved steam

Left 'Manor' Class 4-6-0 No 7808 *Cookham Manor* and 'Modified Hall' 4-6-0 No 6998 *Burton Agnes Hall* with the Great Western Society vintage train stock are seen just beyond Malvern Wells at the approach to Colwall Tunnel. This is Saturday 14 June 1975 and the train is a GWS special from Didcot to Hereford after the Society had gained the first ARPS annual award for an outstanding contribution to voluntary railway preservation. The train was composed of eight carriages, which included the Ocean Saloons Nos 9112 'Queen Mary' and 9118 'Princess Elizabeth'. *PH*

Below 'Castle' Class 4-6-0 No 5051 *Drysllwyn Castle* rounds the curve at the top of Hatton Bank and puts up a magnificently clean exhaust. This was the returning 'Sunset Special', again composed of the GWS vintage train on the first outing for the 'Castle', from Stratford-upon-Avon to Didcot. The date is Saturday 26 January 1980. No 5051 was re-united with its original name in preservation, for from 1937 it was named *Earl Bathurst*. Withdrawal from British Railways had taken place in May 1963 from Llanelly shed. *PH*

Another 'Castle', this time No 4079 Pendennis Castle, leaving Chester with the 'Birkenhead Flyer' Ian Allan special, one of the last Birkenhead to Paddington workings, on Saturday 4 March 1967. Pendennis Castle now resides in Australia. PH

Above Early preservation days at Buckfastleigh on the Dart Valley Railway. The date is Thursday 31 August 1967, and '14XX' Class 0-4-2T No 1420 keeps an auto-coach company. The train is actually stationary and the engine out of steam, but the photograph gives the impression that it is on the move. No 1420 had last worked for British Railways in 1964 and was withdrawn in November at Gloucester Barnwood. *PH*

Below Reviving the days of the mixed freight on the Severn Valley Railway. The date is Saturday 10 April 1976 and the location near Trimpley Reservoir. '57XX' 0-6-0PT No 5764 is the engine making light of the work and delighting the photographers. This engine had been withdrawn from Old Oak Common in May 1960 and sold to London Transport from where it was purchased for preservation. *PH*

A Great Western and LMS combination leaving Church Stretton on a 'Welsh Marches Express' on Saturday 11 April 1981. The leading engine is 'Hall' 4-6-0 No 4930 *Hagley Hall*, and with it Stanier 4-6-0 No 5000. It is interesting to compare the two designs, as Stanier took with him Great Western ideas when he went to the LMS. His 'Black Five' was really the LMS equivalent of the 'Hall'. The ram in the photograph seems totally unimpressed with what is passing! *PH*

Above Stanier 'Jubilee' 4-6-0 No 5690 *Leander* attacks the grade on the approach to Scotby station on the Settle & Carlisle line with a return special on Saturday 26 April 1980. *Leander* had been built in March 1936 and first operated from Crewe North. Withdrawal came in March 1964 from Bristol Barrow Road, and the engine then languished rusting away at Barry Docks until rescued in May 1972. *PH*

Left Hampton Loade on the Severn Valley Railway on Saturday 15 June 1974. Arriving with a train from Bridgnorth is Ivatt '2MT' 2-6-0 No 46443. This engine had been built at Crewe Works and entered traffic on 25 February 1950 at Derby shed. It was withdrawn on 25 March 1967 from Manchester Newton Heath and purchased soon after for preservation. *PH*

The graceful lines of 'Princess Royal' Class 4-6-2 No 6201 *Princess Elizabeth* are beautifully caught in this view near Church Stretton of a 'Welsh Marches Express'. There was still snow on the tops of the hills on the day this photograph was taken, Saturday 14 February 1981. As British Railways No 46201, the engine had been retired from Carlisle Upperby during the week-ended 20 October 1962. *PH*

Above 'B1' 4-6-0 No 1306 *Mayflower* pilots Stanier 4-6-0 No 45407 on the line out from Carnforth on a special to Leeds and then York on Saturday 16 October 1976. The 'B1', which took its name from No 61379, seen on page 124, was withdrawn from Bradford Low Moor on 30 September 1967, the last active member of the Class. *PH*

Left Our last look at steam in action is powerful-looking 'A4' 4-6-2 No 4498 *Sir Nigel Gresley* at Kents Bank, heading north on a Gainsborough Model Railway Society special. The 'A4' had taken over the train at Carnforth and is here opening up after a signal check. The date is Saturday 16 September 1978. *PH*

Appendix

Locomotive allocations, Liverpool Edge Hill: January 1948-February 1967

1 January 1948

Fowler '3MT' 2-6-2T

40006	40050
40007	

Johnson/Fowler '2P' 4-4-0

40495

LMS '2P' 4-4-0

40628

Stanier '4' 2-6-4T

42426	42597
42453	42612
42459	42658
42564	

Stanier '5MT' 4-6-0

44904	45347
44935	45350
44941	45351
45045	45376
45054	45380
45094	45387
45256	45398
45298	45399
45332	45400
45344	45410

Unrebuilt 'Patriot' '6P' 4-6-0

45500 Patriot
45501 St Dunstans
45517
45520 Llandudno
45533 Lord Rathmore
45543 Home Guard
45547

Rebuilt 'Patriot' '7P' 4-6-0

45521 Rhyl
45523 Bangor
45526 Morecambe and Heysham
45527 Southport
45545

'Jubilee' '6P' 4-6-0

45567 South Australia
45586 Mysore
45592 Indore
45613 Kenya
45623 Palestine
45634 Trinidad
45666 Cornwallis
45672 Anson
45673 Keppel
45681 Aboukir
45724 Warspite
45725 Repulse

'Claughton' '5XP' 4-6-0

46004

'Royal Scot' '7P' 4-6-0

46106 Gordon Highlander
46111 Royal Fusilier
46124 London Scottish
46134 The Cheshire Regiment
46135 The East Lancashire
   Regiment
46136 The Border Regiment
46138 The London Irish Rifleman
46144 Honourable Artillery
   Company
46156 The South Wales Borderer
46164 The Artists' Rifleman

Webb '2P' 0-6-2T

46900	46917

LMS '3F' 0-6-0T

47309	47404
47325	47597
47385	47603
47402	47651

LMS '7F' 0-8-4T

47930	47956
47933	47958
47938	47959
47951	

LNWR 'G1'/'G2A' '6F'/'7F' 0-8-0

48898	49155
48908	49239
48927	49242
48933	49287
48966	49333
49016	49355
49032	49385
49130	

LNWR 'G2' '7F' 0-8-0

49449

L&Y Aspinall '2F' 0-6-0ST

51318	51439
51353	51445

L&Y Aspinall '3F' 0-6-0

52111	52170

Webb '2F' 0-6-2T

58887	(27596)
58897	(27674)
58898	(27681)
58900	(7699)
58912	(7751)
58915	(7757)
58922	(7787)
58924	(7791)
58928	(7803)
58930	(7816)
58935	(7833)

Total locomotives allocated: 117

4 November 1950

Fowler '3MT' 2-6-2T

40001	40007
40003	

Stanier '3MT' 2-6-2T

40103	40144

Stanier '4MT' 2-6-4T

42426	42596
42459	42597
42564	42602
42570	42612
42583	

Hughes/Fowler '5MT' 2-6-0

42892	42925

Stanier '5MT' 4-6-0

44768	45256
44769	45276
44772	45303
44906	45333
44907	45343
44941	45347
45005	45350
45017	45352
45113	45376
45181	45380
45242	45393
45243	45398
45248	45399

Unrebuilt 'Patriot' '6P' 4-6-0

45515 Caernarvon
45533 Lord Rathmore
45538 Giggleswick

Rebuilt 'Patriot' '7P' 4-6-0

45521 Rhyl
45527 Southport
45531 Sir Frederick Harrison

'Jubilee' '6P' 4-6-0

45558 Manitoba
45567 South Australia
45596 Bahamas
45613 Kenya
45623 Palestine
45637 Windward Islands
45670 Howard of Effingham
45673 Keppel
45681 Aboukir
45721 Impregnable
45726 Vindictive
45737 Atlas

'Royal Scot' '7P' 4-6-0

46106 Gordon Highlander
46111 Royal Fusilier
46123 Royal Irish Fusilier
46124 London Scottish
46134 The Cheshire Regiment
46135 The East Lancashire
   Regiment
46137 The Prince of Wales's
   Volunteers (South Lancashire)
46138 The London Irish Rifleman
46144 Honourable Artillery
   Company
46153 The Royal Dragoon
46156 The South Wales Borderer
46164 The Artists' Rifleman

'Princess Royal' '8P' 4-6-2

46200 The Princess Royal
46201 Princess Elizabeth
46203 Princess Margaret Rose
46204 Princess Louise
46205 Princess Victoria

LMS '3F' 0-6-0T

47294	47402

47325	47404
47353	47407
47357	47416
47385	47597
47392	

Beames LMS '7F' 0-8-4T

47931	47939

Stanier '8F' 2-8-0

48457	48512
48510	48513

LNWR 'G1'/'G2A' '6F'/'7F' 0-8-0

48898	49200
48932	49224
48933	49239
49082	49301
49126	49355
49137	49392
49173	49394

LNWR 'G2' '7F' 0-8-0

49399	49427
49404	49429
49412	49445
49419	49449

L&Y Aspinall '2F' 0-6-0ST

51353	51445

L&Y Aspinall '3F' 0-6-0

52111	52321
52118	52330

Webb '2F' 0-6-2T

58921	58932

Total locomotives allocated: 124

30 January 1954

Fairburn '4MT' 2-6-4T

42121

Stanier '4MT' 2-6-4T

42426	42583
42459	42596
42564	42602
42570	

Stanier '5MT' 4-6-0

44768	45250
44769	45256
44772	45276
44773	45303
44906	45305
44907	45343
45020	45373
45039	45376
45069	45380
45111	45388
45113	45393
45181	45398
45242	45399
45243	45413
45249	45421

Unrebuilt 'Patriot' '6P' 4-6-0

45515 *Caernarvon*
45518 *Bradshaw*
45533 *Lord Rathmore*
45538 *Giggleswick*
45550

Rebuilt 'Patriot' '7P' 4-6-0

45521 *Rhyl*
45525 *Colwyn Bay*
45527 *Southport*
45531 *Sir Frederick Harrison*
45534 *E. Tootal Broadhurst*

'Jubilee' '6P' 4-6-0

45567 *South Australia*
45596 *Bahamas*
45606 *Falkland Islands*
45613 *Kenya*
45623 *Palestine*
45670 *Howard of Effingham*
45681 *Aboukir*
45721 *Impregnable*

'Royal Scot' '7P' 4-6-0

46123 *Royal Irish Fusilier*
46124 *London Scottish*
46135 *The East Lancashire Regiment*
46149 *The Middlesex Regiment*
46152 *The King's Dragoon Guardsman*
46153 *The Royal Dragoon*
46158 *The Loyal Regiment*
46164 *The Artists' Rifleman*

'Princess Royal' '8P' 4-6-2

46200 *The Princess Royal*
46204 *Princess Louise*
46205 *Princess Victoria*
46207 *Princess Arthur of Connaught*
46208 *Princess Helena Victoria*

LMS '3F' 0-6-0T

47325	47411
47353	47416
47357	47487
47385	47489
47392	47498
47402	47519
47404	47597
47407	

Stanier '8F' 2-8-0

48260	48512
48457	48513

LNWR 'G2A' '7F' 0-8-0

48932	49314
49082	49355
49137	49368
49173	49375
49200	49392
49224	49394

LNWR 'G2' '7F' 0-8-0

49399	49427
49404	49429
49412	49434
49419	49437
49423	49445

L&Y Aspinall '2F' 0-6-0ST

51313	51445
51353	

L&Y Aspinall '3F' 0-6-0

52140	52321

Total locomotives allocated: 115

30 January 1960

Fairburn '4MT' 2-6-4T

42121	42155

Stanier '4MT' 2-6-4T

42459	42570
42564	42583

Stanier '5MT' 4-6-0

44768	45181
44769	45242
44772	45249
44773	45281
44906	45376
44907	45399
45005	45401
45032	45413
45039	45421
45069	

Unrebuilt 'Patriot' '6P' 4-6-0

45515 *Caernarvon*
45516 *The Bedfordshire and Hertfordshire Regiment*
45518 *Bradshaw*

Rebuilt 'Patriot' '7P' 4-6-0

45521 *Rhyl*
45525 *Colwyn Bay*
45527 *Southport*
45531 *Sir Frederick Harrison*
45535 *Sir Herbert Walker KCB*

'Jubilee' '6P' 4-6-0

45552 *Silver Jubilee*
45554 *Ontario*
45560 *Prince Edward Island*
45567 *South Australia*
45578 *United Provinces*
45583 *Assam*
45586 *Mysore*
45596 *Bahamas*
45613 *Kenya*
45670 *Howard of Effingham*
45678 *De Robeck*
45681 *Aboukir*
45704 *Leviathan*
45733 *Novelty*

'Royal Scot' '7P' 4-6-0

46114 *Coldstream Guardsman*
46119 *Lancashire Fusilier*
46124 *London Scottish*

'Princess Royal' '8P' 4-6-2

46203 *Princess Margaret Rose*
46204 *Princess Louise*
46208 *Princess Helena Victoria*
46211 *Queen Maud*

LMS '3F' 0-6-0T

47285	47487
47289	47488
47336	47498
47353	47519
47357	47566
47402	47594
47404	47597
47412	47656
47416	

Stanier '8F' 2-8-0

48152	48457
48249	48509
48280	48512
48318	48513
48433	48683

LNWR 'G2A' '7F' 0-8-0

48927	49224
49064	49243
49082	49375
49137	49392
49144	49394
49173	

LNWR 'G2' '7F' 0-8-0

49399	49416
49404	49434
49405	49437
49412	

L&Y Aspinall '2F' 0-6-0ST

51445

Class '40' 1-Co-Co-1 diesel

D215	D223
D218	D231
D220	D234
D222	D236

Class '08' 0-6-0 diesel shunter

D3578   D3579

Total allocation:
Steam locomotives 100
Diesel locomotives 10

5 October 1963

Hughes/Fowler '5MT' 2-6-0

42815	42920
42848	42924
42851	42925
42886	

Stanier '5MT' 4-6-0

44768	45069
44769	45094
44772	45156*
44773	45187
44838	45188
44864	45242
44906	45249
44907	45284
44964	45307
45005	45312
45015	45376
45039	45440
45041	

* named *Ayrshire Yeomanry*

Rebuilt 'Patriot' '7P' 4-6-0

45531 *Sir Frederick Harrison*

'Royal Scot' '7P' 4-6-0

46119 *Lancashire Fusilier*

'Princess Coronation' '8P' 4-6-2

46229 *Duchess of Hamilton*
46233 *Duchess of Sutherland*
46241 *City of Edinburgh*
46243 *City of Lancaster*

LMS '3F' 0-6-0T

47285	47487
47289	47519
47349	47566
47357	47594
47416	

Stanier '8F' 2-8-0

48078	48457
48152	48512
48188	48513
48249	48652
48280	48742
48323	48746
48433	

Class '40' 1-Co-Co-1 diesel

D215 *Aquitania*
D223 *Lancastria*
D231 *Sylvania*
D234 *Accra*
D234 *Apapa*
D290
D305
D306
D309
D312
D343

Class '03' 0-6-0 diesel shunter

D2198   D2373

Class '08' 0-6-0 diesel shunter

D3019	D3579
D3370	D4154
D3578	D4155

Total allocation:
Steam locomotives 60
Diesel locomotives 19

5 November 1966

Stanier '5MT' 4-6-0

44666	45005
44717	45015
44768	45039
44772	45069
44773	45094
44774	45156*
44837	45187
44838	45242
44863	45249
44864	45284
44906	45307
44907	45376
44926	45426
44933	45440
44964	

* named *Ayrshire Yeomanry*

LMS '3F' 0-6-0T

47357	47493
47406	

Stanier '8F' 2-8-0

48056	48433
48152	48467
48178	48513
48249	48528
48258	48536
48293	48743
48308	48746
48371	

Class '08' 0-6-0 diesel shunter

D3019	D3836
D3370	D3858
D3578	D4154
D3579	D4155

Total allocation:
Steam locomotives 47
Diesel locomotives 8

7 October 1967

Stanier '5MT' 4-6-0

44772	45005
44773	45055
44777	45133
44834	45156*
44838	45187
44864	45284
44906	45287
44907	45375
44926	45376
44933	45426
44964	

* by this date the nameplates
were removed

Stanier '8F' 2-8-0

48012	48374
48017	48433
48056	48467
48119	48529
48124	48665
48268	48687
48293	48692
48294	48696
48308	48746
48371	

Class '08' 0-6-0 diesel shunter

D3019	D3858
D3370	D3950
D3578	D4147
D3579	D4154
D3836	D4155

Total allocation:
Steam locomotives 40
Diesel locomotives 10

6 May 1960
(day of closure)
also showing distribution
of the locomotives

Stanier '5MT' 4-6-0

44711	Withdrawn
44777	To 9H Patricroft
44864	Withdrawn
45055	To 9H Patricroft
45156*	To 9H Patricroft
45187	To 9H Patricroft
45282	Withdrawn
45284	Withdrawn
45287	To 9H Patricroft
45305	To 10D Lostock Hall

* re-named *Ayrshire Yeomanry*
with wooden nameplates

Stanier '8F' 2-8-0

48045	Withdrawn
48056	Withdrawn
48124	Withdrawn
48293	To 10D Lostock Hall
48294	To 10D Lostock Hall
48374	To 9H Patricroft
48467	To 9H Patricroft
48529	To 9D Newton Heath
48614	Withdrawn
48665	To 9D Newton Heath
48687	To 9D Newton Heath
48692	To 9K Bolton
48715	To 10F Rose Grove
48722	Withdrawn
48746	To 9D Newton Heath
48752	To 10F Rose Grove

Class '08' 0-6-0 diesel shunter

D3019	D3858
D3370	D3950
D3578	D4147
D3579	D4154
D3836	D4155

All to 8J Allerton

Locomotives withdrawn from Liverpool Edge Hill, 1948-1968

Number and type	Withdrawn (week-ended date)

Stanier '4MT' 2-6-4T

42599	29 September 1962

Hughes/Fowler '5MT' 2-6-0

42815	26 September 1964
42851	30 May 1964
42920	26 December 1964
42925	28 November 1964

Stanier '5MT' 4-6-0

44666	18 February 1967
44688	20 August 1966
44711	4 May 1968
44717	26 August 1967
44768	27 May 1967
44769	26 June 1965
44772	4 November 1967
44773	16 December 1967
44774	26 August 1967
44827	3 July 1965
44834	9 December 1967
44837	9 September 1967
44838	9 March 1968
44863	6 May 1967
44864	4 May 1968
44906	2 March 1968
44907	4 November 1967
44926	20 April 1968
44933	14 October 1967
44964	14 October 1967
45005	27 January 1968
45015	16 September 1967
45039	26 August 1967
45069	24 June 1967
45094	25 February 1967
45103	10 October 1964
45133	3 February 1968
45242	3 June 1967
45244	3 August 1963
45249	10 December 1966
45282	4 May 1968
45284	4 May 1968
45296	10 February 1968
45307	7 October 1967
45375	27 January 1968
45376	30 March 1968
45395	23 March 1968
45401*	11 November 1961
45414	6 February 1965
45426	23 March 1968
45440	16 September 1967

* the first Stanier 4-6-0 to be withdrawn

Unrebuilt 'Patriot' '6P' 4-6-0

45513	15 September 1962
45520	19 May 1962
45524	15 September 1962
45533	15 September 1962
45547	15 September 1962
45551	16 June 1962

'Jubilee' '6P' 4-6-0

45637	13 December 1952

'Claughton' '5XP' 4-6-0

46004*	23 April 1949

* the last of its class to be withdrawn

'Royal Scot' '7P' 4-6-0

46119	16 November 1963

'Princess Royal' '8P' 4-6-2

46204	7 October 1961
46208	20 October 1962

'Princess Coronation' '8P' 4-6-2

46229	15 February 1964
46233	8 February 1964
46241	5 September 1964
46243	12 September 1964

Fowler '2F' 0-6-0T

47166	11 May 1963

LMS '3F' 0-6-0T

47285	21 August 1965
47349	25 July 1964
47353	17 February 1962
47357	24 December 1966
47404	24 February 1962
47406	24 December 1966
47407	19 December 1959
47411	19 December 1959
47412	28 September 1963
47415	16 April 1966
47416	25 June 1966
47485	9 January 1965
47487	21 August 1965
47488	1 December 1962
47489	19 December 1959
47493	31 December 1966
47519	2 October 1965
47594	11 July 1964

Beames LMS '7F' 0-8-4T

47930	7 August 1948
47931*	15 December 1951
47932	17 September 1949
47933	10 June 1950
47936	11 June 1949
47937	7 October 1950
47938	21 February 1948
47939	2 December 1950
47951	22 January 1949
47956	27 November 1948
47958	4 December 1948
47959	5 June 1948

* the last of its class to be withdrawn

Stanier '8F' 2-8-0

48012	30 March 1968
48017	4 November 1967
48045	4 May 1968
48056	4 May 1968
48078	28 August 1965
48119	2 December 1967
48124	4 May 1968
48129	19 March 1966
48152	25 March 1967
48178	12 November 1966
48188	14 May 1966
48249	10 December 1966
48258	26 August 1967
48268	28 October 1967
48280	7 May 1966
48308	13 April 1968
48362	23 December 1967
48371	14 October 1967
48395	9 September 1967
48433	6 April 1968
48450	30 September 1967
48512	24 September 1966
48513	18 March 1967
48528	5 August 1967
48536	21 January 1967
48604	29 April 1967
48614	27 April 1968
48696	30 December 1967
48722	11 May 1968
48743	25 March 1967

(48729: This Wigan Springs Branch engine was withdrawn on 14 October 1967 and cut up at Edge Hill shed due to the serious damage it sustained after running away with a coal train on the 'Gridiron' and crashing into 4-6-0 No 44933.)

LNWR 'G1'/'G2A' '6F'/'7F' 0-8-0

48927	11 November 1961
48933	16 December 1950
49037	29 December 1962
49038	3 April 1948
49064	4 June 1960
49082	15 October 1960
49114	1 December 1962

49116	14 November 1959
49130	1 December 1962
49132	18 April 1959
49137	7 October 1961
49144	10 November 1962
49155	26 May 1962
49200	28 March 1959
49216	24 November 1962
49224	1 December 1962
49237	31 December 1949
49243	11 March 1961
49293	1 December 1962
49333	20 May 1950
49352	15 September 1962
49355	14 November 1959
49366	17 October 1959
49375	8 December 1962
49377	27 October 1962
49392	14 October 1961
49394	27 October 1962

LNWR 'G2' '7F' 0-8-0

49399	14 October 1961
49404	28 April 1962
49405	14 October 1961
49412	7 October 1961
49415	1 December 1962
49416	1 September 1962
49419	7 November 1959
49427	7 November 1959
49429	14 November 1959
49432	1 December 1962
49434	20 October 1962
49435	14 November 1959
49437	1 September 1962
49444	7 October 1961
49445	14 November 1959

L&Y Aspinall '2P' 2-4-2T

50692	8 October 1949

L&Y Aspinall '2F' 0-6-0ST

51313	27 October 1956
51353	22 June 1957
51441	18 March 1961
51445	18 June 1960

L&Y Aspinall '3F' 0-6-0

52105	25 April 1953
52111	10 March 1951
52170	18 September 1948
52321	27 February 1954
52330	15 December 1951

LNWR Webb '2F' 0-6-2T

58883	31 December 1949
58898	2 October 1948
58922	31 July 1948

Liverpool Edge Hill shed visits, 1948-1967

On shed
Sunday 4 April 1948
3.00 pm

Fowler '3MT' 2-6-2T

40006	8A
40007	8A

LMS Compound '4P' 4-4-0

41163	6A Chester

Stanier '4P' 2-6-4T

42426	8A
42453	8A
42459	8A
42564	8A
42597	8A
42612	8A
42638	24E Blackpool
42643	23A Accrington
42658	8A

Hughes/Fowler '5MT' 2-6-0

42734	26B Agecroft

Stanier '5MT' 2-6-0

42947	5B Crewe South

Stanier '5MT' 4-6-0

44808	5A Crewe North
44935	8A
45041	5B Crewe South
45109	8B Warrington
45134	5B Crewe South
45238	25B Huddersfield
45332	8A
45344	8A
45347	8A
45376	8A
45380	8A
45416	12B Carlisle Upperby

Unrebuilt 'Patriot' '6P' 4-6-0

45500	8A
45533	8A
45542	5A Crewe North
45547	8A

Rebuilt 'Patriot' '7P' 4-6-0

45521	8A
45523	8A
45526	8A

'Jubilee' '6P' 4-6-0

45586	8A
45592	8A
45613	8A
45623	8A
45672	8A
45678	12B Carlisle Upperby
45686	5A Crewe North

'Claughton' '5P' 4-6-0

46004	8A

'Royal Scot' '7P' 4-6-0

46106	8A
46111	8A
46135	8A
46136	8A
46138	8A
46144	8A
46170	1B Camden

'Princess Royal' '8P' 4-6-2

46205	8A

Webb '2P' 0-8-2T

46900	8A
46917	8A

LMS '3F' 0-6-0T

47309	8A
47325	8A
47376	8B Warrington
47385	8A
47402	8A
47404	8A
47597	8A
47603	8A

Beames LMS '7F' 0-8-4T

47930	8A
47931	8A
47932	8A
47933	8A
47939	8A
47951	8A
47956	8A
47958	8A
47959	8A

Stanier '8F' 2-8-0

48407	19C Canklow
48490	18A Toton
48734	5B Crewe South
48745	5B Crewe South
48753	5B Crewe South

LNWR 'G1'/'G2A' '6F'/'7F' 0-8-0

48898	8A
48908	8A
48927	8A
49065	8C Speke Junction
49071	8D Widnes
49130	8A
49237	8A
49239	8A
49242	8A
49287	8A
49355	8A

LNWR 'G2' '7F' 0-8-0

49449	8A

L&Y Aspinall '2P' 2-4-2T

50692	8A
50695	8A

L&Y Aspinall '2F' 0-6-ST

51353	8A
51445	8A

LNWR Webb '2F' 0-6-2

58883 (27580)	8A
58887 (27596)	8A
58897 (27674)	8A
58898 (27681)	8A
58900 (7699)	8A
58912 (7751)	8A
58915 (7757)	8A
58922 (7787)	8A
58924 (7791)	8A

Total locomotives present: 98
Visitors 23
Home-based 75

Note: No locomotives had been re-numbered into their British Railways numbers.

On shed
Sunday 20 March 1955
2.15 pm

LMS Compound '4P' 4-4-0

41121	8A

Stanier '4MT' 2-6-4T

42426	8A
42450	6A Chester
42564	8A
42570	8A
42602	8A
42664	8A

Hughes/Fowler '5MT' 2-6-0

42887	9A Longsight

Stanier '5MT' 2-6-0

42949	8E Brunswick

Ivatt '4MT' 2-6-0

43114	19A Sheffield Grimesthorpe

Stanier '5MT' 4-6-0

44712	2A Rugby
44715	2A Rugby
44757	20A Leeds Holbeck

44769	8A
44906	8A
44907	8A
44949	25B Huddersfield
45005	8A
45039	8A
45041	5B Crewe South
45242	8A
45243	8A
45249	8A
45252	8B Warrington
45314	10A Wigan Springs Branch
45372	2A Rugby
45376	8A
45380	8A

Unrebuilt 'Patriot' '6P' 4-6-0

45515	8A
45516	8A
45518	8A
45550	8A

Rebuilt 'Patriot' '7P' 4-6-0

45525	8A

'Royal Scot' '7P' 4-6-0

46110	8A
46124	8A
46149	8A
46152	8A
46153	8A
46157	8A

'Princess Royal' '8P' 4-6-2

46200	8A
46205	8A
46208	8A

'Princess Coronation' '8P' 4-6-2

46250	1B Camden
46251	8A

LMS '3F' 0-6-0T

47353	8A
47357	8A
47385	8A
47392	8A
47404	8A
47407	8A
47416	8A
47487	8A
47489	8A
47498	8A
47597	8A

Stanier '8F' 2-8-0

48078	20C Royston
48512	8A

LNWR 'G2A' '7F' 0-8-0

48932	8A
49130	8A
49173	8A
49224	8A
49355	8A

LNWR 'G2' '7F' 0-8-0

49399	8A
49404	8A
49419	8A
49423	8A
49427	8A
49429	8A
49437	8A

L&Y Aspinall '2F' 0-6-0ST

51313	8A
51353	8A

L&Y Aspinall '3F' 0-6-0

52140	8A

Standard '4MT' 4-6-0

75012	6G Llandudno Junction
75035	6A Chester

Total locomotives present: 74
Visitors 16
Home-based 58

On shed
Sunday 2 September 1962
3.00 pm

Fairburn '4MT' 2-6-4T

42121	8A
42155	8A

Stanier '4MT' 2-6-4T

42442	26F Patricroft
42599	8A

LMS '4F' 0-6-0

44424	5D Stoke

Stanier '5MT' 4-6-0

44768	8A
44906	8A
44907	8A
44911	9B Stockport Edgeley
45005	8A
45015	8A
45039	8A
45041	8A
45196	8B Warrington
45242	8A
45248	5B Crewe South
45376	8A
45446	5A Crewe North

Rebuilt 'Patriot' '7P' 4-6-0

45535	8A

'Jubilee' '6P' 4-6-0

45695	55C Farnley Junction

'Royal Scot' '7P' 4-6-0

46116	5A Crewe North

'Princess Royal' '8P' 4-6-2

46208	8A

'Princess Coronation' '8P' 4-6-2

46233	8A

Fowler '2F' 0-6-0T

47166	8A

LMS '3F' 0-6-0T

47336	8A
47357	8A
47412	8A
47416	8A
47487	8A
47488	8A
47519	8A
47566	8A
47594	8A
47656	8A
47657	8B Warrington

Stanier '8F' 2-8-0

48152	8A
48157	55A Leeds Holbeck
48188	8A
48249	8A
48280	8A
48297	8C Speke Junction
48323	8A
48714	26F Patricroft
48746	8A
48752	21D Aston

LNWR 'G2A' '7F' 0-8-0

49037	8A
49114	8A
49130	8A
49142	8A
49144	8A
49173	8A
49224	8A
49293	8A
49352	8A
49375	8A
49377	8A

LNWR 'G2' '7F' 0-8-0

49415	8A
49432	8A
49434	8A
49448	8A

WD 'Austerity' '8F' 2-8-0

90219	24B Rose Grove

Class '46' diesel

D173	8A (on loan)

Class '40' diesel

D231	8A
D328	5A Crewe North

Class '03' 0-6-0 diesel shunter

D2373	8A
D2393	8A

Class '08' 0-6-0 diesel shunter

D3579	8A

LMS 0-6-0 diesel shunter

12017	8C Speke Junction

Total locomotives present: 68
Visitors 16
Home-based 52

On shed
Sunday 20 June 1965
2.30 pm

Stanier '5MT' 4-6-0

44768	8A
44769	8A
44773	8A
44819	8B Warrington
44827	8A
44834	8A
44864	8A
44906	8A
44907	8A
44937	12B Carlisle Upperby
44964	8A
45015	8A
45018	12A Carlisle Kingmoor
45034	8C Speke Junction
45054	10A Carnforth
45069	8A
45096	9J Agecroft
45132	6J Holyhead
45187	8A
45239	9K Bolton
45242	8A
45284	8A
45293	12A Carlisle Kingmoor
45440	8A

'Jubilee' '6P' 4-6-0

45590	8B Warrington
45633	8B Warrington
45697	55A Leeds Holbeck

Ivatt '2MT' 2-6-0

46424	8C Speke Junction

LMS '3F' 0-6-0T

47285	8A
47357	8A
47415	8A
47416	8A
47487	8A

Stanier '8F' 2-8-0

48129	8A
48152	8A
48163	8A
48188	8A
48249	8A
48280	8A
48512	8A
48742	8A

Standard '9F' 2-10-0

92059	8B Warrington
92092	8H Birkenhead
92158	8C Speke Junction

Class '03' 0-6-0 diesel shunter

D2392	8A

Class '08' 0-6-0 diesel shunter

D3019	8A
D3578	8A
D3579	8A
D4155	8A

Class '11' 0-6-0 diesel shunter

12081	8C Speke Junction

Total locomotives present: 50
Visitors 17
Home-based 33

On shed
Sunday 19 February 1967
12.00 pm

Stanier '5MT' 4-6-0

44682	5D Stoke
44717	8A
44768	8A
44772	8A
44773	8A
44838	8A
44864	8A
44933	8A
44964	8A
45015	8A
45039	8A
45069	8A
45094	8A
45156	8A
45284	8A
45324	9F Heaton Mersey
45376	8A

45426	8A	48119	8A
45440	8A	48124	8A
		48152	8A

Ivatt '2MT' 2-6-0

		48249	8A
46503	8C Speke Junction	48371	8A
		48395	8A

LMS '3F' 0-6-0T

		48433	8A
		48513	8A
47566	Withdrawn from	48536	Withdrawn
	Aintree	48687	8A
		48696	8A

Stanier '8F' 2-8-0

		48743	8A
48045	8A		
48056	8A		

Standard '5MT' 4-6-0

73140   9H Patricroft

Standard '9F' 2-10-0

92054	8C Speke Junction
92071	12A Carlisle Kingmoor
92078	8B Warrington
92082	8H Birkenhead
92091	8C Speke Junction
92104	8H Birkenhead
92153	8C Speke Junction
92227	8B Warrington

Class '47' Co-Co diesel

D1654   86A Cardiff Canton

Class '05' 0-6-0 diesel shunter

D2567   8C Speke Junction

Class '08' diesel shunter

D3019	8A
D3836	8A
D3858	8A
D4154	8A
D4155	8A

Total locomotives present: 51
Visitors 15
Home-based 36

Index of locations